KU-013-765

I DREAM A WORLD

REVISED EDITION

A 10TH ANNIVERSARY CELEBRATION

THE LIBRARY
NEW COLLEGE
SWINDON

I DREAM A WORLD

Portraits of Black Women Who Changed America

Revised & Enlarged Edition

THE LIBRARY
NEW COLLEGE
SWINDON

Photographs and interviews by
Brian Lanker

Edited by Barbara Summers

Revised edition edited by Yvonne Easton

Foreword by Maya Angelou

Stewart, Tabori & Chang

New York

Page 1: detail, portrait of Myrlie Evers.
Page 2: portrait of Leontyne Price.

"I Dream a World" is the title of a poem by Langston Hughes.

Images made possible through the generosity of the Professional Photography Division, Eastman Kodak Company.

Photographic prints by Gary Schneider of Schneider/Erdman, New York, New York

Copyright © 1989 Brian Lanker

All rights reserved. No portion of this book may be reproduced, stored in a retrieval system, or transmitted in any form or by any means, mechanical, electronic, photocopying, recording, or otherwise, without written permission from the publisher.

Published in 1999 by
Stewart, Tabori & Chang
115 West 18th Street
New York, NY 10011
www.abramsbooks.com

Library of Congress has cataloged the original edition as follows:
Library of Congress Cataloging-in-Publication Data
Lanker, Brian.
    I dream a world.
    Includes index.
    1. Afro-American women—Portraits. 2. Afro-American women—
Interviews   I. Summers, Barbara   II. Title.
E185.86.L355   1989   305.1´8896073   88-32697
ISBN   1-55670-888-2 (cloth)
ISBN   1-55670-923-4 (paper)

Printed in China

10 9 8 7 6 5 4 3 2

More than 450,000 copies in print

Book design by Jeff Batzli
Cover design by Melanie Random

The publisher would like to thank Mari Evans, who has granted permission to reprint an extract from "I Am a Black Woman" on page 10 of this book.

Stewart, Tabori & Chang is a subsidiary of

LA MARTINIÈRE GROUPE

for Lynda,
Julie, Jacki, Dustin,
and Priscilla,
with love

Editor's Note

The challenge of editing *I Dream a World* was tremendous. I was invited into the lives of seventy-five magnificent women through interviews, photographs, and research materials created and collected by Brian Lanker, who had stepped through the looking glass—outside race, gender, age, and class. My job—the privilege and pain of it—was to capture a life on a page of words. A page seemed a meager space for the wealth of events and observations each woman had to share.

Reading through the transcripts of these interviews was like reading a natural literature, books of real-life adventure. In dialogue, Brian queried with an intellect as sensitive and probing as his eye. The talk was rich. Each woman had her language, her accent, her own speed and breathing. I could hear the thinking unfolding. I could feel sudden remembrance surface in crystalline expression.

The refining process treated words as valuable individual weights. Accurate tone, mood, and moral balance were important. Time, tense, and potential shifted constantly. Each woman spoke from a unique moment in her life. But the page took on a life of its own far beyond that moment.

For lack of space, we had to leave out many stories: poignant ones, like Leah Chase's memories of giving one's best even in the midst of poverty, and perversely dramatic ones, like that of the young Ellen Stewart being viciously punished when she showed up to claim a prize she had won by mail in a fashion design contest. We let go of many philosophical one-liners, short on words but long on experience, from Charlayne Hunter-Gault—''I think it's terrific to aim higher than you can possibly reach''—to Marva Collins—''Our children are what they are taught just as we are what we eat.'' Often the abundance of rich anecdotes forced us to leave good material on the cutting room floor.

It was very easy to see how *history* developed from observation through editing, carving flesh-and-blood heroes in stone. But as they spoke, the women of *I Dream a World* demanded that we record *herstory*, a different version of who the fittest were that survived, how they did it and why. I appreciated their openness, especially that of the grand older sisters who revealed heart and mind, although not all and not all of the time, to a young white man enthusiastic with his discovery.

Looking at these women, love is not hard to find. It pokes out in a pencil behind Miss Ruby Forsythe's ear, leaving her two hands free to hold a child apiece. It is woven into the kente cloth of Dr. Niara Sudarkasa's academic robes. It wafts with beauty and sadness across the profile of the Lady Lena Horne. And love shelters all who come within Mother Hale's arms.

Love was not hard to find in their words, either. It seemed to be a key to their success. A truly beautifying discovery for me was to find so much love in anger. It was a fist-up, death-defying love that challenged the unfair conditions of life and muscled in on injustice as it nursed both sides of a nation.

Valiant and vulnerable, these women were there. To re-create them as vividly as possible on the page and on their own terms was the challenge of life to literature.

—BARBARA SUMMERS

Contents

Editor's Note
8

They Came to Stay by Maya Angelou
10

Preface
12

Portraits
19

They Came to Stay

I
am a black woman
tall as a cypress
strong
beyond all definition still
defying place
and time
and circumstance
    assailed
        impervious
           indestructible
Look
    on me and be
renewed

—from ''I Am a Black Woman,''
Mari Evans

Black women whose ancestors were brought to the United States beginning in 1619 have lived through conditions of cruelties so horrible, so bizarre, the women had to re-invent themselves. They had to find safety and sanctity inside themselves or they would not have been able to tolerate those tortuous lives. They had to learn to be self-forgiving quickly, for often their exterior exploits were at odds with their interior beliefs. Still they had to survive as wholly and healthily as possible in an infectious and sick climate.

Lives lived in such cauldrons are either obliterated or forged into impenetrable alloys. Thus, early on and consciously, Black women as reality became possibilities only to themselves. To others they were mostly seen and described in the abstract, concrete in their labor but surreal in their humanness.

They knew the burden of feminine sensibilities suffocated by masculine responsibilities.

They wrestled with the inescapable horror of bearing pregnancies which could only result in issuing more chattels into the rapacious maw of slavery.

They knew the grief of enforced separations from mates who were not theirs to claim, for the men themselves did not have legal possession of their own bodies.

And men, whose sole crime was their hue,
the impress of their Maker's hand,
and frail and shrinking children too
were gathered in that mournful band.

—from *The Slave Auction*,
Frances Ellen Watkins Harper

The larger society, observing the women's outrageous persistence in holding on, staying alive, thought it had no choice save to dissolve the perversity of the Black woman's life into a fabulous fiction of multiple personalities. They were seen as acquiescent, submissive Aunt Jemimas who showed grinning faces, plump laps, fat embracing arms, and brown jaws pouched in laughter. They were described as leering buxom wenches with round heels, open thighs, and insatiable sexual appetites. They were accused of being marauding matriarchs of stern demeanor, battering hands, unforgiving gazes, and castrating behavior.

When we imagine women inhabited by all those apparitions, it becomes obvious that the women themselves did not hallucinate, but rather that they were national, racial, and historical hallucinations. Those contradictions stump even the most fertile imagination, for they could not have existed despite the romantic racism which introduced them into the American psyche. Surprisingly, above all, many women did survive as themselves. In this book we meet them, undeniably strong, unapologetically direct.

The photographer, Brian Lanker, possesses an acute eye and a brave heart. He has discovered women whose images show us the high cost of living and the rich reward of thriving. Lanker intends to capture the viewer with the twin magic of his camera and the women's faces. These women regard us, understand us, gaze through us into a beyond, alien to our most common view. Each seems to know something we have not known. The sameness of their gaze informs us that they will not be removed, that indeed although they are shaken, bruised, and uprooted, they are determined to remain.

This foreword does not mean to be an explanation of the Black woman's stamina. Rather, it is a salute to her as an outstanding representative of the human race. Here, in this book, educators, athletes, dancers, judges, politicians, artists, actresses, writers, singers, poets, and social activists dare to look at life with humor, determination, and respect. Their visages do not entertain hypocrisy. To those who would desire chicanery, the honesty of these women is terrifying.

The heartbreaking tenderness of Black women *and* their majestic strength speak of the heroic survival of a people who were stolen into subjugation, denied chastity, and refused innocence.

These women have descended from grandmothers and great-grandmothers who knew the lash firsthand, and to whom protection was a phantom known of but seldom experienced. Their faces are captured here for the ages to regard and wonder, but they are whole women. Their hands have brought children through blood to life, nursed the sick, and folded the winding cloths. Their wombs have held the promise of a race which has proven in each challenging century that despite threat and mayhem it has come to stay. Their feet have trod the shifting swampland of insecurity, yet they have tried to step neatly onto the footprints of mothers who went before. They are not apparitions; they are not superwomen. Despite their majestic struggle they are not larger than life. Their humanness is evident in their accessibility. We are able to enter the photographs and enter into the spirit of these women and rejoice in their courage and nearness.

Precious jewels all. Thanks to their persistence, art, sublime laughter and love we may all yet survive our grotesque history.

—MAYA ANGELOU

Preface

My life for the past two years has been spent in the living rooms, offices, kitchens, and backyards of some of the finest people it has ever been my privilege to encounter, seventy-five extraordinary individuals who allowed me to enter their homes and their hearts. My hope is that this project will allow readers and viewers to see something of those lives and feel the strength of those hearts for a brief moment, and to be informed by them and inspired by them as I have.

I have often been asked, Why this project? Why would a white male set out to document the lives of seventy-five black women? It is a result of my own growing awareness of the vast contribution black women have made to this country and society, a contribution that still seems to have gone largely unnoticed. As a photojournalist, I felt the need to prevent these historical lives from being forgotten. Many of the women opened ''the doors'' and many advanced America through the modern civil rights and women's movements. Three people in particular mark turning points in the development of my desire to embark on this project—Barbara Jordan, Alice Walker, and Priscilla Williams.

I remember as if it were yesterday sitting in front of the television screen listening and watching Barbara Jordan deliver her speech to the Democratic National Convention in 1976, and coming away saying, ''Why isn't she running for president?'' She was the person I wanted to see in the White House. Sometime later I ran across a quotation from a speech she gave before the House of Representatives. In many ways it sums up my feelings about this project.

''We, the people.'' It is a very eloquent beginning. But when that document was completed on the seventeenth of September in 1787, I was not included in that ''We, the people.'' I felt somehow for many years that George Washington and Alexander Hamilton just left me out by mistake. But through the process of amendment, interpretation, and court decision I have finally been included in ''We, the people.''

Barbara Jordan's political ideas were so strong that I not only wanted to include her in this project, I wanted the privilege of meeting her.

In 1982 I read *The Color Purple* by Alice Walker. Her fiction opened my eyes to the reality of the lives that some women have lived. I realized that while white male society was driving down the boulevard of opportunity with only an occasional traffic light to contend with, these women often reached their goals by traveling a circuitous path adjacent to that boulevard, a pathway cluttered with the obstacles of racism, poverty, sexism, and more, making their route all but impassable. Her writing brought me out of my own narrow world and into the world of black women. When I finished reading, my world was not the same.

During the 1970s and 1980s, I developed a close friendship with Priscilla Williams, a remarkable human being who had helped in my wife's upbringing. When I think of Priscilla, I'm reminded of a line from a Langston Hughes poem of a mother talking to her son. She says, ''Life for me ain't been no crystal stair.'' These words address Priscilla's difficulties in life too, and yet she added crystal to our home with her laughter and her love. By sharing some of the struggles from her own life, she taught me and my family a lot about survival, strength, dignity, and love.

My own awareness of racism in our society evolved gradually because my childhood was generally sheltered from it. But my naivete was met head-on when I saw the civil rights movement come to life in my living room on television. I had no prior inkling that America was consumed by bigotry. In my innocence, I thought that Abraham Lincoln had made everyone equal. I had spent years with my hand over my heart believing, "One nation, under God, indivisible, with liberty and justice for all." So when the glowing box in our living room disrupted all that I'd been taught, I was shocked. Black people were being attacked by dogs, clubs, and fire hoses. I was bewildered. My mother had instilled in us the belief that everyone was equal in the eyes of God. Didn't God tell everyone?

When I went to college in the mid-sixties, there were black people in all my classes and some in my circle of friends. The newspaper articles I continued to read made the struggles in the South seem worlds away from my pluralistic, southwestern campus.

It was during this time I met a friend who would loom large in my life and in this project. He is Allen Dutton, who was my college photography instructor. He spent little time teaching me about f-stops and shutter speeds. Instead he attempted to open my world and sensitize me to the deeper emotions of both myself and my photographic subjects. He asked that I use the camera as a probe—not only as a recorder of obvious visual information—so that the resulting

photograph might reveal more of the inner essence of the individual. I've strived to do this ever since.

Several years later when I was working for the *Phoenix Gazette*, I received the real history lesson. As in many other cities in America, riots protesting poor living conditions broke out in the housing projects of Phoenix and I was assigned to photograph them. I vividly remember how I and another photographer, in the middle of the night, crouched for cover behind a short wall for protection, while bullets from a sniper's gun were ricocheting off a metal fence behind us. Meanwhile, on a nearby balcony several stories up was a woman in curlers, dressed in a bra and khaki shorts, who danced to the words and music of Aretha Franklin, "R-E-S-P-E-C-T . . . respect just a little bit . . ." I thought it was a civil rights song and didn't find out until years later that the lyrics were the words of a woman appealing to her man. Though it was a life-threatening experience, I remember thinking at the time, Yes, she deserves respect, more than the little bit Aretha was pleading for.

Until the seventies, I was like most every other man I knew as far as sexism was concerned. It took the women's movement of that era and a failed marriage to enlighten me. Having children was no less informative, as I came face to face with the fact that I wanted no less for my daughters than I did for my son.

As I lived through these times and felt the sting of racism and sexism, I realized that it was possible to fight for freedom for black people but not necessarily for women. It was indeed possible to fight to liberate women, but not black people. Black women knew the binds of bigotry and the chains of chauvinism and sought release from both.

In their lifetimes, the women in this book saw changes come to pass. Many pioneered the way and opened door after door. These were women who took a mighty step across the stage of America.

My first task when I embarked on this project was to come up with a list of women to include. One could fill volumes and museums with candidates, so wide is the historical scope. Writers alone, of which several are portrayed, could fill their own volume. From a wealth of individuals, I drew up an initial list of perhaps twenty-five people who immediately came to mind and then headed off to the Black Studies sections of various libraries for research material. I found that some of the women I knew to be notable had little representation in these sections. You soon realize who wrote the history books. It wasn't women.

For two years, John Frook, former News Editor of *LIFE* magazine, scanned dozens of newspapers from around the nation for possible candidates. Yvonne Easton of *LIFE* made countless trips and spent untold hours digging through files at the Schomberg Center in Harlem. The extensive files of Time Inc. were made available by Pat Ryan of *LIFE*, and Yvonne also used them extensively.

Perhaps the best research network was formed by the women themselves. Their lives and experiences reached deeper than any library shelves. Some, such as Marian Wright Edelman, expanded the project's scope by recommending individuals who otherwise almost certainly would have been overlooked. Organizations such as the National Coalition of 100 Black Women and the National Council of Negro Women went out of their way to help in our research.

When all was said and done, only a few women declined to participate. Ella Fitzgerald could not participate because of her health. Aretha Franklin agreed to be included but couldn't find the time.

When I met each woman, I proceeded first with the interview, which gave us a chance to get to know each other. I had no set list of questions, but I was interested in each person's childhood and family. I asked about their earliest experiences with racism and sexism, and which seemed the more prevalent in their experience. What did they do to combat discrimination, given the legality of much of it until the reforms of the sixties? Were they hopeful for more progress in their lifetimes? I was interested in their success, their art—and their failures as well. But I also let the interviews, which averaged three hours, go where the women wanted to take them. I discovered a world of wit and wisdom, and philosophies of work and life.

Next came the challenge of bringing that world and my new-found understanding of the woman into the photograph. This is always the hardest part. Normally the portraits were taken on the next day, in a session that lasted anywhere from thirty minutes to several hours. The amount of time spent photographing didn't usually have a direct influence on the success of the photograph. Where it took several hours for just the right light for the portrait of Rosa Parks, it took just a few brief minutes for everything to come together with Septima Clark.

As the project progressed, an assumption I had made did not hold up. Though I wanted to come into these women's lives, I was not sure they would care to open their worlds and sometimes fragile pasts to me. I was pleased and surprised that not once in the course of two years of work was I ever left feeling alienated or distant because of my race and gender.

I had also anticipated that the road for many of these women had been hard, but I was not prepared for the full brunt of that harshness. I was often left shocked by their experiences. There were times when some reached deep into their past, recalling some of the most painful memories of all. Tears were shared, but much laughter was shared as well.

The outpouring of generosity was wonderful too. I remember visiting Leah Chase, the Creole chef extraordinaire. After we had completed an early-morning photographic session, she sat my two assistants and me down to a breakfast feast of sautéed quail with plum jelly, a Creole veal dish, spicy sausage, cheese grits, scrambled eggs, two different catfish dishes, homemade biscuits, herbed tomatoes—and I'm sure I'm leaving out two more dishes. Her love and culinary expertise flowed freely.

I had the privilege of two separate visits with Maya Angelou, who honored me by writing the book's foreword. From my research, I knew how tal-ented she was in so many diverse areas, but I was constantly surprised how she would excuse herself from the work at hand and moments later pull a truly delicious home-cooked meal out of a hat.

As I think about the women I've met through this project, it strikes me how many of them grew up in strong, supportive families with the black church playing a major role. Though others outside their families or communities were quick to try to limit their world, their experiences inside the home instilled in them the conviction that they were not to be limited by anything. They were told they could do anything they chose if they only set their mind to it and worked hard. They were free to dream and were often driven to fulfill their dreams.

In fact, all of the women in this book have dreamed of a world not only better for themselves but for generations to come, a world where character and ability matter, not color or gender. As they dreamed that world, they acted on those dreams and they changed America.

This celebration of sisters is not an attempt to elevate or lower any segment of society, it is merely an opportunity to savor the triumphs of the human spirit, a spirit that does not speak only of black history. My greatest lesson was that this is my history, this is American history.

—BRIAN LANKER

A 10th Anniversary Celebration

On a spring morning in 1988, I hurried down a corridor of Harlem Hospital's facility for the aged looking for Anna Arnold Hedgeman, a former mayoral cabinet member of New York City. Recently widowed and ill, she could no longer live an independent life. My mission, as researcher and cultural consultant for the *I Dream A World* project, was to convince Mrs. Hedgeman to become a participant in the forthcoming book and exhibit. I didn't want to be late.

As I neared my destination, I heard loud voices that didn't get any lower when I appeared in the doorway of Anna Hedgeman's room. She was sitting in a wheelchair, waving her cane to make a point, dressed just as she is in her portrait. The other voice belonged to Jean Blackwell Hutson, her old and dear friend of fifty years, who was standing and listening at the moment that I arrived. She was leaning on her cane while Anna finished with a grand flourish. Mrs.Hutson didn't look serious, which was a relief to me—with no hospital personnel in sight, what would I have done had the women begun fencing? Seizing the moment, I introduced myself and shared my impression with them. We all had a good laugh at the vision I had con-jured in my mind, and later, both women agreed to participate in the project.

That meeting was my first encounter with the qualities of spirit, will, and humor I found embodied in the African-American women responding to the call of *I Dream A World*. Later, I met fifty-three of its seventy-six subjects at a private celebration, prior to the exhibit's premier at Washington D.C.'s Corcoran Gallery in 1989. Women of determination, integrity, and dignity energized the room. Awed and touched by the emotion of the moment, my eyes filled as I saw Wilma Rudolph embrace Mother Clara Hale; women were recognizing and hugging each other all around me, some of them meeting for the first time. The exhibit's opening had brought them together in the flesh, but the book linked them in a timeless sister-hood. After all, they were the black women who had changed America.

Coming of age in a Harlem-based family of women made me keenly aware of the black woman's fight for respect and equality. So when the opportunity came to work with Brian Lanker on *I Dream A World,* I knew what a book like that could mean. I had a grandmother who had been a suffragette. Her mother had been a slave, and my grandmother herself was a domestic worker. I had first-hand knowledge of the effects of racism and sexism, but I also witnessed the change in African-American life during World War II. Black women left white America's domestic arena to work in the war industries for a fair wage. At the end of the war, change was in the air and it was clear that black women would be at its vanguard. Witness Septima Poinsette Clark, Mrs. Rosa Parks, Constance Baker Motley in the 1950s; Angela Davis and Barbara Jordan in the 1960s and 1970s; and Oprah Winfrey in the 1980s, more powerful than ever in the 1990s.

I Dream A World answers a great need. Women's and Black Studies departments in American universities and colleges use it consistently as a text; public school systems, grasping its import, use it to teach civics, mathematics, geography, and history. Moreover, *I Dream A World* is a universal experience: Women of color in the diaspora recognize themselves and identify with it. I saw and heard this when I traveled with the exhibit around America and overseasmeeting and speaking with those who came to view the photographs. Each country has its own cadre of sisters vital to its growth, candidates for an indigenous version of *I Dream A World*.

As editor of this 10th anniversary edition, I contacted the women still alive, to announce the coming of this commemorative printing and to ask for their latest news. They were delighted with mine and responded accordingly. Although sixteen of the *I Dream A World* sisterhood died during the intervening years, their images imprint an age, and the lessons of their lives are timeless.

I Dream A World established a cultural meeting point for racial and sexual polarities in America and it created a new page in American history books where succeeding generations can write their names. If that's not changing America, I don't know what is.

—YVONNE EASTON

I DREAM A WORLD

Portraits

Rosa Parks

Born February 4, 1913, in Tuskegee, Alabama

When Rosa Parks refused to give up her seat on a Montgomery, Alabama, bus in 1955, her arrest sparked a 381-day bus boycott that ignited the Civil Rights Movement. Fired from her tailoring job, she moved to Detroit, Michigan, where she was a special assistant to Congressman John Conyers for twenty-five years. She founded the Rosa and Raymond Parks Institute for Self-Development, inaugurated in 1988. In 1996, she was awarded the Presidential Medal of Freedom, the nation's highest civilian honor, by President Clinton. A museum and library that will bear her name is scheduled to open in Montgomery, Alabama.

Rosa Parks stands in Martin Luther King, Jr.'s Dexter Avenue Baptist Church, where the historic bus boycott was organized.

As far back as I can remember, being black in Montgomery we were well aware of the inequality of our way of life. I hated it all the time. I didn't feel that, in order to have some freedom, I should have to leave one part of the United States to go to another part of the same country just because one was South and one was North.

My mother believed in freedom and equality even though we didn't know it for reality during our life in Alabama.

In some stores, if a woman wanted to go in to try a hat, they wouldn't be permitted to try it on unless they knew they were going to buy it, or they put a bag on the inside of it. In the shoe stores they had this long row of seats, and all of those in the front could be vacant, but if one of us would go in to buy, they'd always take you to the last one, to the back of the store. There were no black salespersons.

At the Montgomery Fair [a department store] I did men's alterations. Beginning in December coming up to the Christmas holiday, the work was a bit heavy. When I left the store that evening, I was tired, but I was tired every day. I had planned to get an electric heating pad so I could put some heat to my shoulder and my back and neck. After I stepped up on the bus, I noticed this driver as the same one who had evicted me from another bus way back in 1943.

Just back of the whites there was a black man next to one vacant seat. So I sat down with him. A few white people boarded the bus and they found seats except this one man. That is when the bus driver looked at us and asked us to let him have those seats. After he saw we weren't moving immediately, he said, "Y'all make it light on yourselves and let me have those seats."

When he saw that I was still remaining in the seat, the driver said, "If you don't stand up, I'm going to call the police and have you arrested." I said, "You may do that."

Two policemen came and wanted to know what was the trouble. One said, "Why don't you stand up?" I said, "I don't think I should have to." At that point I asked the policemen, "Why do you push us around?" He said, "I don't know, but the law is the law and you're under arrest."

The decision was made by the three of us, my husband, my mother, and me, that I would go on and use my case as a test case, challenging segregation on the buses.

When I woke up the next morning and realized I had to go to work and it was pouring down rain, the first thing I thought about was the fact that I never would ride a segregated bus again. That was my decision for me and not necessarily for anybody else.

People just stayed off the buses because I was arrested, not because I asked them. If everybody else had been happy and doing well, my arrest wouldn't have made any difference at all.

The one thing I appreciated was the fact that when so many others, by the hundreds and by the thousands, joined in, there was a kind of lifting of a burden from me individually. I could feel that whatever my individual desires were to be free, I was not alone. There were many others who felt the same way.

The first thing that happened after the people stayed off was the black cab companies were willing to just charge bus fare instead of charging cab fare. Others who had any kind of car at all would give people rides. They had quite a transportation system set up. Mass meetings were keeping the morale up. They were singing and praying and raising money in the collection to buy gasoline or tires.

There was a lot of humor in it, too. Somebody told a story about a [white] husband who had fired the family cook because she refused to ride the bus to work. When his wife came home, she said, "If you don't go get her, you better be on your way." Some white people who were not wanting to be deprived of their domestic help would just go themselves and pick up the people who were working for them.

The officials really became furious when they saw that the rain and bad weather or distance or any other problem didn't matter.

Many whites, even white Southerners, told me that even though it may have seemed like the blacks were being freed, they felt more free and at ease themselves. They thought that my action didn't just free blacks but them also.

Some have suffered much more than I did. Some have even lost their lives. I just escaped some of the physical—maybe not all—but some of the physical pain. And the pain still remains. From back as far as I can remember.

When people made up their minds that they wanted to be free and took action, then there was a change. But they couldn't rest on just that change. It has to continue.

It just doesn't seem that an older person like I am should still have to be in the struggle, but if I have to be in it then I have no choice but to keep on.

I've been dreaming, looking, for as far back as I had any thought, of what it should be like to be a human being. My desires were to be free as soon as I had learned that there had been slavery of human beings and that I was a descendant from them. If there was a proclamation setting those who were slaves free, I thought they should be indeed free and not have any type of slavery put upon us.

Janet Collins

Born March 7, 1917, in New Orleans, Louisiana

I come from a very unique family, exceedingly proud of their background. They never allowed us to have an inferiority complex. In fact, they were arrogant. I had to overcome arrogance.

I asked about some aristocrat in the family. "Who is this Marquis de Lavallade?" I said. They told me, "That man could have been some old reprobate who was kicked out of France. We don't need to be proud of that."

When I was about fifteen, I auditioned for the famous Ballet Russe de Monte Carlo. I saw ballet dancers warming up backstage at the Philharmonic. They gathered on this winding staircase. One had beautiful red shoes on that I will never forget, red high-heeled shoes.

Léonide Massine [the choreographer] called us one by one. When my turn came there was a hush in that place like you wouldn't believe. I was the only little black face around. When I finished the ballerinas applauded.

Massine saw talent. He told me, "You would make a wonderful character dancer. The only trouble is, in order for you to belong to the company, I would have to paint you white. You wouldn't like that, would you?"

Those were the terms. I said, "No, I wouldn't want that." So I thanked him and went out on the library steps, and I will never forget, I cried, cried, and cried. I thought talent mattered, not color. That's why I cried.

When I went home and told Aunt Adele, she said, "You get back to the barre and start your exercises. Don't try to be good, be excellent. Don't let that stop you."

I won the Donaldson Award for being the finest dancer on Broadway [in 1951 in Cole Porter's *Out of This World*]. I could see Broadway was a charade. I could see the fickleness—the happiness and the cruelty. At the top the air is very light but it is cruel. The top is not forever. Either you walk down or you are going to be kicked down. I walked down.

The reason I became ballerina of the Metropolitan Opera was because I couldn't be topped. You don't get there *because*, you get there *in spite of*.

My favorite move? I love the air. I was a jumper. I was an adagio dancer from when I was about fifteen. It's very athletic dancing that takes the girl and swings her around very spectacularly. I made the mistake of telling Zachary Solov, the Metropolitan Opera's bright young choreographer, that I had done adagio dancing and sometimes he almost never let me get out of the air!

The Met had never seen a black face. Marian Anderson couldn't get in there. I felt like a doorknob. I was the dancer who opened the door.

The Metropolitan Opera was going on tour. Mr. Rudolph Bing, the General Manager of the Metropolitan Opera, called me into his office one day and he was very uncomfortable. He said "Miss Collins, I do not like what I have to tell you, but I am not Abraham Lincoln." He said he could not take me south on tour because there was a law down there that blacks and whites could not appear on the same stage together.

I tried to speak to an old friend, but she put me on a pedestal. I just wanted to talk and she said, "Oh, you are not like the rest of us. You are Sunday and we are everyday."

Your own family can do that to you. Always asking what are you doing next, and we have read so and so, and we are collecting your reviews. But never, "Are you lonely? How do you feel?"

When you get to be an exceptional black, you don't belong to the white and you don't belong to the black. You are too good for the black and you will always be black to the white.

Art serves me. I don't serve it. But I have to be a servant before it serves me. In other words, I have to be disciplined. There is no such thing as freedom without discipline. The one who is free is disciplined.

A vertical line is dignity. The horizontal line is peaceful. The obtuse angle is action. That's universal, it is primary.

I used every gift God gave me. The gift of love is the greatest. It's a difficult thing because there are people I know that I can't stand. But love doesn't mean affection. It means treating them justly even when they are terrible people. That takes a bit of doing, an awful lot of Grace.

Janet Collins, prima ballerina, was the first black artist to perform on the stage of the Metropolitan Opera House in New York City. Her 1951 debut in Aida *was preceded by her winning of the 1950–51 Donaldson Award for best dancer in a Broadway musical. She remained with the Metropolitan's corps de ballet until 1954, dancing in* Carmen *and* Samson and Delilah. *After touring the United States and Canada in solo dance concerts, she taught at several colleges and dance institutions in New York and California before retiring to Seattle to paint. Dance remains an influence, as she strives to achieve movement in her paintings, which revolve around religious subjects.*

Eva Jessye

Born January 20, 1895, in Coffeyville, Kansas
Died February 21, 1992, in Ann Arbor, Michigan

Eva Jessye, as choral director for the first Broadway production of George Gershwin's Porgy and Bess *in 1935, was credited with authenticating the sound of this American classic. She was the first black woman to win international distinction as the director of a professional choral group, the Eva Jessye Singers. Other innovative productions for which she was choral director include* Hallelujah, *the 1929 film by King Vidor, and the Virgil Thomson opera* Four Saints in Three Acts *(libretto by Gertrude Stein). For many years the Ambassador of the Arts from Kansas, she eventually retired to her home in Ann Arbor, Michigan.*

I could read music so easily. The fact is, I didn't have to read the music. The teachers would never let me hear them play 'cause I would just have it. I could always remember. It came naturally to me, not second nature but first nature.

We didn't have no radio, no television, no anything like that, not even a piano for a long, long time. I think I had about the first piano of a black person in Coffeyville.

When I was in school at Kansas Wesleyan University, I heard Booker T. Washington say one day in a lecture, "You go to school, you study about the Germans and the French, but not about your own race. I hope the time will come when you study black history, too. Never forget to sing the songs of your mothers and fathers."

Will Marion Cook was my mentor. He was a composer and an orchestra man. He had what they call a sweet syncopation orchestra that played sweet jazz, ragtime. They called him Daddy Cook. He was so cantankerous, he wouldn't let you change any note on his music.

I went through things in New York. I was living upstairs and my little studio always had little concerts and things. A man knocked on my door and said, "I'm from the electric company and I've been sent time and time again to cut off your electricity. But I stood out here and you were playing so beautifully, I couldn't do it."

In New York at the radio they used to say, "Well, we don't have any need for your music." They thought the Negro didn't know anything except spirituals. Radio was an area black people hadn't broken into and it hadn't been opened for them.

In 1929 I went to Hollywood where we did *Hallelujah*. That was some experience.

King Vidor [the director] fired me. But then they found the boy replacing me couldn't handle the music, couldn't get the results. I had a contract. A lawyer advised me to sit right beside the doorway every morning so they couldn't say I didn't show up.

When they got ready to do some of those big church scenes with two hundred people, I knew how to put little moans and groans and things that would make it real, you know. Vidor was a Southern white man, never looked a black man in the face. He said, "Something don't sound right. What is it?" He missed a fellow who had a beautiful voice that could sound so mournful.

In 1935, I had been traveling with my choir in South Carolina and we got back to New York just in time to audition for *Porgy and Bess*. I had sixteen singers. When we sang, George [Gershwin] said, "That's it, that's what I want." So they were the official choir of the first recorded production and I was the first choral conductor for *Porgy and Bess*.

It's a masterful work. He was definitely gifted, of course, and a lovely person to know. I sat beside him while he was working on some of it in the penthouse on 72nd Street in New York City. He had two pianos downstairs, neck-to-neck concert pianos, and one upstairs that he worked at. (I'm going to add to the Ten Commandments: Thou shall not envy thy neighbor's Steinway pianos.)

George Gershwin knew a great deal, he studied a great deal, but I've been black longer than he has. I had a lot of fun saying that. I was black all day and he wasn't. No imitator can be as close to a thing as one who is the source.

I made a lot of changes when we did *Porgy and Bess*. The producers would ask me, "Do you think it should be this way or that way?" I'd have to go through the score and point out where I thought they went a little astray. But of course, his stuff sounds quite white. You could almost tell he got it from someone else.

Most black people know how to sing the blues. They twist a song all around. That's the black way of singing. Be inventive. They get the most emotion out of a note or a phrase.

I traveled with *Porgy and Bess* to Vienna, Berlin, London, different places in the world, the South Pacific, Australia, Russia. Nothing reaches the mind and deepens the spirit like contact with people.

I used to have an awful time traveling with my group. White people didn't want to accommodate you. I never thought it would be like it is now.

I wonder, why did I keep the sixteen singers touring in two cars, when danger was involved and there was uncertainty about money. At the end of the week we would just share the money. What you were born to do, you don't stop to think, should I? could I? would I? I only think, will I? And, I shall.

I traveled and made money and I wouldn't let anybody get between me and my music. If I belong to anything, I belong to my music, that's all. Any woman of that time would have had the same trouble I had. They never thought a woman could be as devoted to one idea as a man.

They say you should not suffer through the past. You should be able to wear it like a loose garment, take it off and let it drop.

Bertha Knox Gilkey

Born March 18, 1949, in Sanfran, Arkansas

Bertha Gilkey has been an activist for welfare and tenant rights since the age of fourteen. In the mid-1970s she organized the tenants of a deteriorated public housing complex to regain control of their community and their destiny. She was instrumental in obtaining over $30 million in federal funds for renovation and new construction in the Saint Louis area. Founder and president of Urban Women, Inc., a consulting firm that provides leadership and management training to tenant groups, she travels throughout the United States, Europe, and Africa.

They used to call the tenement housing where my mother lived the quadroon. It had no floor, it was all dirt floor and the windows were made out of, like, wax paper. We had no hot and cold running water. We used to get our water from the hydrant. All the people that lived in a quadroon had outside toilets.

Poor to us never meant being irresponsible, not being accountable. Poor always meant you were held accountable for what you did and you had standards.

When we moved to Cochran, we thought we were moving to heaven, to finally have hot and cold running water. Cochran was beautiful. When Cochran was all white, they didn't refer to it as a project. It was called Cochran Gardens. As Cochran became more and more black, I began to see the services reduced. Once it became all black, there was no standards. It moved from being a neighborhood to a project. It became a dumping ground.

My mother had fifteen children living in a three-bedroom apartment. There was no recreation. There was nothing to do. There was nowhere for kids to go. There was no jobs, no nothing. Everything was removed and we were left to eat each other or get eaten.

I watched women—black women and poor white women—struggle to make a community, a neighborhood, with nothing. Then I watched millions of dollars come from the antipoverty programs. After we did all the legwork, the people that were hired to work the programs were men, not women. It meant the programs were designed based on their philosophy, not the philosophy of women. And public housing is woman-dominated.

In 1974 the city voted, the housing authority and the mayor said to tear Cochran down. We said, ''Over our dead bodies. We're here through all the bad times and we're gonna be here for the good times.''

When we took over managing Cochran in 1976, out of 880 units only 400 units were occupied. All the rest were vacant, had been vacant for almost nine, ten years. Two managers had gotten shot here before we took over managing.

I remember many days I used to stand downstairs and beg people not to move out of Cochran. We wouldn't have lights and in the winter the heater wouldn't heat and the pipes would burst all over. And they said, ''Bertha, we just cannot stay.'' And I would say, ''It's gonna get better.''

I took the gang leaders, second and third offenders, and created renovation crews. Kids that were normally vandalizing, setting these units on fire, were now restoring them.

We changed the people before we changed the building.

Cochran is clearly a revolution of its own. It was supposed to fail because tenants don't manage; we are managed. We employ almost two hundred people. We control our own destiny, we control how we live, how our children live, the quality of life our children will get. To me that's revolution. And what I like about it, I don't go to jail today. I get put on TV.

It's frustrating that people today say that Cochran only works because of the charisma of Bertha Gilkey. Charisma doesn't stop people from urinating in alleys. Charisma doesn't stop vandalism. Charisma doesn't stop junkies from selling dope openly. It's not charisma that makes Cochran work. It's because we gave people back a vested interest in where they live.

When people say that black girls are having babies too young, I say that my mother had her first child at eleven. Black women have always had babies young. That's not the reason for the crime and the devastation that is happening in the black community. There has to be morality and accountability and responsibility put back into our communities. And that can only be done by us, by the people.

Who's raising black men in this country? Black women. So if black men are not being very conscious of black women, then it is our fault. I think black women tend to love our sons and raise our daughters. We tend to not give men responsibility, not hold them accountable the way we hold our daughters.

What worked in the sixties doesn't work in the eighties so I changed my hair, pressed it right, put on a dress. . . . My blackness has never been in my hair. Blackness is not a hair style. It is not a dashiki. Judge my blackness by the jobs that we have, by the money we are able to generate in the community in advance of the support services. Judge my blackness by that.

The one thing I learned real quick, once I took off my rebel clothes, was that there is big money in poor folks. There's millions of people that benefit. They eat because I'm poor. They never want to eliminate poverty. They just want to control it. The day they eliminate poverty, they go out of business.

I've always picketed in front of the White House, never went inside. But I was invited to go inside for the signing of this bill which will give tenants the right to manage their property and to own if they choose to go to the next step.

Alice Walker

Born February 9, 1944, in Eatonton, Georgia

Alice Walker won the Pulitzer Prize for Fiction and the American Book Award for her third novel, The Color Purple, *published in 1983. Subsequently made into an Oscar-nominated movie,* The Color Purple *intensified discussion among black men and women about image, role, and reality. In 1996, she wrote an emotionally revealing book entitled,* The Same River Twice: Honoring the Difficult—A Meditation on Life, Spirit, Art, and the Making of the Film The Color Purple, Ten Years Later. *The author of twenty-two books, Walker published* Anything We Love Can Be Saved: A Writer's Activism, *in 1997, and a novel,* By the Light of My Father's Smile, *in 1998.*

It was very clear always that my parents were pretty much equal. I think in some ways my father was more intelligent, whereas my mother was more deeply spiritual. He was the one that was good at math. And she was the one really good at art in the way she redesigned the shacks that we lived in, planted gardens, made clothes and quilts, and really created beauty.

No matter what the controversy is about what women are saying and doing, there is a possibility that men will hear. I just hope they don't all get hardening of the sensitivities and sensibilities, as my father did later in his life. I think he was wiped out by being really, really poor.

There is a crying need in our community for reconciliation. Not just between men and women, but generationally, between the daughters and the fathers.

My family is not a reading family. My mother had never read a novel. In a way, it took Steven Spielberg's film for my family to actually read the novel. I think it was the first time that they really felt that they were reading about something they knew. And they loved it.

During childhood I wasn't aware that there was segregation or that it was designed to make me feel bad. White people just seemed very alien and strange to me. I knew that when they appeared everybody sort of stopped having fun, and waited until they left to become alive again. I think as a child you tend to notice that deadening effect on life, more than you would their color.

I was forced to leave Spelman College. I was a rebel, without knowing or planning. I wanted to be myself and I could not do that while thinking about whether my seams were straight, and my hair was straight, and my dress was ironed, and my slip wasn't showing. The administration made it clear that if we were arrested in political demonstrations, we could be expelled. They were on the side of the system, even though we were trying to change apartheid in the South.

[After graduating from Sarah Lawrence and working in the Welfare Department in Brooklyn,] I went to Mississippi and I started working in the movement. I developed educational materials for Head Start programs. I met my former husband, my daughter's father, who was a law student, and we actually desegregated a number of facilities just by ourselves.

There we were, working in Mississippi. I had a baby in one hand and my novel in the other. My husband's car had a bullet hole right through the front windshield and we were just really alone. We were on the frontier. When I found Zora Neale Hurston, it was like seeing that we've always been on the frontier, and that we're really at home there.

If I had not gone and lived in Mississippi and had instead gone to live somewhere else where I could be free, I would never have been free. Now I can live anywhere. I have no guilt. I don't feel like I left something undone. I had to face up to the system that had almost done me in and had done in my father and so many of my people.

I was there for the March on Washington in 1963. I wouldn't have missed it for the world. It was one of those days when you feel the tide is turning and you are with the tide. I heard every word, and every word went through my whole body and through my whole soul: There was such love and vision.

I love this land. I'm not crazy about the nation.

This is a suicidal society. We're poisoning the earth, the air, the water. People are poisoned by their medicines. There's a real inability on the part of the white males that we have elected to understand any kind of interrelatedness. And that's fatal.

I really don't relate to television anymore. Part of it is just the refusal to have trash dumped on me. I'm always amazed that people will actually choose to sit in front of the television and just be savaged by stuff that belittles their intelligence.

I've met Rosa Parks and Fannie Lou Hamer. They have been tempered in the fire of experience, and they have come through whole and shining, and just to be in their presence is to feel the warmth of the shine. They are like jewels. We're rich because we have those women. And I don't mean just black people are rich. I mean human beings are rich because of those women.

It's so clear that you have to cherish everyone. I think that's what I get from these older black women, that sense that every soul is to be cherished, that every flower is to bloom. That is a very different world view from what we've been languishing under, where the thought is that the only way I can bloom is if I step on your flower, the only way I can shine is if I put out your light.

I feel safe with women. No woman has ever beaten me up. No woman has ever made me afraid on the street. I think that the culture that women put out into the world is safer for everyone. They don't put out the guns, they don't encourage the shooting. If you value your life, whether you're a man or woman, if you had a choice, you would choose the culture that lets you live, rather than the culture that is killing you.

I couldn't be a separatist, a racial one, and I can't be a sexual separatist. It just seems to me that as long as we are both here, it's pretty clear that the struggle is to share the planet, rather than to divide it.

Cicely Tyson

Born December 19, 1933, in New York, New York

Whatever good I have accomplished as an actress I believe came in direct proportion to my efforts to portray black women who have made positive contributions to my heritage. What attracted me to acting was the realization that this extremely shy person could suddenly speak. I could express my emotions through someone else. I did not set out to become a role model. I did set out to become the best possible actress I could be. My careful choice of roles came as a direct result of the type of negative images that were being projected of black people throughout the world, particularly of black women. I knew deep within me that I could not afford the luxury of just being an actress—I had something to say as a member of the human race, black and female.

The gift of portraying Jane Pittman afforded me the privilege of interviewing several black women ranging from the ages of ninety-seven to one-hundred and five. One of the women, in recalling her life, told me how wonderful it was growing up in the South. This was a woman who was taken away from her parents at the age of six and sent to work. I sat there looking at this remarkable face, scarred with the ravages of life—those eyes, that voice—the pain was agonizing.

Role model? My mother leads the pack. When I think of the price she paid for "this life," I regard her as I do all of the other black women throughout history: miraculous. They are miracles in this human race. Somehow they are always at the bottom of the ladder, the last rung. And somebody is always trampling on their fingers. Yet despite the pain, the bruises and the bleeding, they did not let go. They hung on for as long as they could and when they felt they had rallied enough strength from within to reach for the next rung, they did. Those are the role models!

This constant reminder by society that I am "different" because of the color of my skin, once I step outside of my door, is not my problem—it's theirs. I have never made it my problem and never will. I will die for my right to be human—just human.

When we were children (there were three of us—my brother, my sister, and myself), among the many things Mama taught us was embroidery. She would buy these huge things, tablecloths, bedspreads—whatever—and she would give each of us a corner to work (the fourth corner was hers). "When I get back," she would say, "I want you to have finished this much right here." Today we each have several of these beautiful pieces—remembrances of Mama's efforts to keep her family harmonious.

I say that if each person in this world will simply take a small piece of this huge thing, this tablecloth, bedspread, whatever and work it regardless of the color of the yarn, we will have harmony on this planet.

Cicely Tyson has portrayed many heroic women on stage, screen, and television, and her courageous choice of roles has had an impact far beyond her individual career. She won two Emmy awards in 1974 for her portrayal of Jane in The Autobiography of Miss Jane Pittman, *and she was nominated for an Oscar in 1973 for her role as Rebecca in the feature film* Sounder. *She holds a record seven Image Awards from the NAACP. Ms. Tyson earned her seventh Emmy nomination for her co-starring role in the television series* Sweet Justice, *and won her third Emmy for the mini-series* The Oldest Living Confederate Widow Tells All. *In 1998, she starred in the title role of the television adaptation of Alex Haley's story,* Mama Flora's Family.

31

Katherine Dunham

Born June 22, 1909, in Joliet, Illinois

Katherine Dunham redesigned the art of modern dance in the 1930s by introducing elements from African and Caribbean folk cultures. Dancer, choreographer, anthropologist, teacher, writer, and initiate of Haitian vodun, she reached a broad and enthusiastic audience. She performed in original theatrical revues, the 1940 Broadway musical, Cabin in the Sky, *and in seven films, among them the 1943 production of* Stormy Weather. *In the late 1960s, she relocated to East Saint Louis, Illinois. There, at the Katherine Dunham Centers for Arts and Humanities, she is chief choreographer, as well as arts administrator, visionary, and social justice activist. She received the Kennedy Center Honors in 1983, and the Scripps American Dance Festival Award in 1986.*

It was in me to dance and I had to do it to be satisfied. This need for motion, for physical expression, comes to the fore. I think many parents don't want their children to dance. But it's a stronger drive than even parental pressure.

Dance can free people from some of their oppressions. Just by using the body in its rhythmic patterns, it heightens circulation. Then if you work hard enough, so that water is running off you, there is a purifying process in dancing. There *should* be.

Out of the WPA [Works Progress Administration] we developed a large company of all sizes and ages. I constructed a ballet around the small village I had lived in in Martinique while on a Rosenwald grant. As I worked with the dancers, I got to feel great responsibility for them. I could see, constantly, the need for socializing, for educating, as well as absorbing the music and atmosphere and learning the steps.

I felt that our production, which was as near perfect as I could make it, portrayed a part of black people that had not been seen on the stage or in theater. I had returned from field work and I felt that's what anthropology had done for me.

I finally agree with Martha Graham when she said that I was the high priestess of the pelvic girdle. When people saw us using the central part of the body with dignity, beauty, and some authenticity, I think it struck them, and relieved them.

I never thought of myself as sexy. I didn't think of what we were doing on the stage as sexy, because I could always feel and know that there was something solid, that authentic feeling under it.

I did not separate a physical act from its cultural context, from its spiritual meaning. So if I would do a thing like winding my hips, the movement was perfectly natural. You go to a nightclub and you see somebody grind and bump. The purpose is to arouse the audience sexually and it shows in the quality of movement.

You can get rhythmic motion in an athlete, but it's the choreography that makes it dance. Dunham technique has evolved from the study of primitive rhythms in dance with percussion as a base.

We stayed in over fifty countries. My husband, John Pratt, was white, my secretary was white, and the company manager would book me into a hotel, which assumed I was white. In Cincinnati, the manager of the hotel asked me if I would move. I said no and the whole thing went on. Next thing, he sent up a big bruiser. I said, "What are you here for?" He said he was here to take me bodily out of the room. It was hot, the window was up. So I sat on the sill and put one leg over. I said, "All right, you come. You come and I will go out this window"—it happened to be high up—"and I have a witness that you pushed me out." Well, he blanched. Then he turned around and left.

Your daring has to be backed up with a willingness to lose that point. To make a bigger point, you might have to lose one.

I like to avoid confrontations if I can. But if I cannot, I want to be totally prepared to solve them or eliminate them, one way or another.

Why East Saint Louis and why Haiti? They have so much in common. At first when I went, I had never seen oceans and palm trees and all that sort of thing. I loved it. I still love Haiti. It has problems and East Saint Louis has problems. But both places have their structure. The family is very strong. I like that because it's probably the only salvation for young people. I used to be amused at the young militants because if something had to be done on Sunday morning, whatever it was, waylaying something or a Molotov cocktail or something going on, if the grandmother said, "You go to church this morning," they would go.

My years of activity with the militants in East Saint Louis, I think, come from a drive to try to bring about social justice.

Our program is socialization through the arts. I see it as taking the rough edges off of their lives and trying to channel them into ways of thinking and behaving that will help them in other parts of the world.

I think that break dancing grew out of a need on the part of street youth to express themselves physically. It's almost like overcoming gravity, overcoming all of the obstacles. You don't just turn twelve times like Nureyev, you turn twenty-four times.

In knowing how to overcome little things, a centimeter at a time, gradually when bigger things come, you're prepared. You're not taken by surprise, you're not even angry or upset. It just rouses your spirit to do more.

I've had arthritis since I can remember. I have been a guinea pig for more experiments on arthritis than anybody.

It was a continuous deterioration, until finally I was just dancing on bones against bones.

If you dance, you dance because you have to. Every dancer hurts, you know.

Barbara Jordan

Born February 21, 1936, in Houston, Texas
Died January 17, 1996, in Austin, Texas

When I was a student at Texas Southern University in Houston, I had to ride the bus from my house to school across town. There was a little plaque on the bus near the back that said "Colored" and when I'd get on I'd have to go all the way back to that little plaque and I was passing empty seats all the time.

In 1962, I lost a contest for the state House of Representatives. And some of the people were saying that I probably lost the race because people are just not accustomed to voting for a woman. And I just said, "Well, now, that is totally ridiculous and I'll just have to try to alter that."

All my growth and development led me to believe that if you really do the right thing, and if you play by the rules, and if you got enough good, solid judgment and common sense, that you're going to be able to do whatever you want to do with your life. My father taught me that.

The civil rights movement called America to put a giant mirror before it and look at itself. I believe that the movement said to America, "Look at what you have been saying to us black people all of these years. Look what you have been trying to sell us as the bill of goods for America. Look at that and then ask yourselves, have you really done it? Do the black people who were born on this soil, who are American citizens, do they really feel this is the land of opportunity, the land of the free, the home of the brave, all that great stuff?"

And when America looked into that giant mirror and heard these questions, the drumbeat—that's what the movement was, this drumbeat of questions—America had to say, "No, I really haven't, as a country, lived up to what I've said this country would be for you." And so the civil rights movement was a time of requiring that America be honest in its promises. And that was the goodness of the movement.

I am telling the young people that if you're dissatisfied—and I don't think they can be students in a school of public affairs and not be dissatisfied—if you are dissatisfied with the way things are, then you have got to resolve to change them. I am telling them to get out there and occupy these positions in government and make the decisions, do the job and make it work for you.

There seems to be a chilling of opportunity rather than an enlivening and enhancing of opportunity. But to me, that should just be the spark that energizes you to get out there and do things.

How do you communicate to young people that you do better, your opportunity is expanded and enhanced if you're educated? That's the message I know many teachers out there are trying to deliver now, but it's a drumbeat which must continue. The drop-out rate is criminal.

We've got to bring a new kind of literacy and it's not going to be easy and it is going to cost money. But I say that we need first to develop the will to try to do something. Can we afford it? We have to.

Things which matter cost money, and we've got to spend the money if we do not want to have generations of parasites rather than generations of productive citizens.

It is the linkage of humanity which has to solve the problem. Yes, these kids are perhaps predominantly black or brown or whatever, but they are human. And I say to the whites that you are being very shortsighted to say they're not your kids. They are your kids because we are all representative of everybody else. That is the human linkage.

It is a burden of black people that we have to do more than talk. We have somehow got to sacrifice our lives as an example to move young people along so that they will understand that it is a long, slow, tough road to really make it so that it lasts. I have got to offer myself as a role model to others so that perhaps something in my life will help move a young black person who might otherwise drop out to stay in school. That is part of my mission.

I define morality as adherence to the Golden Rule, "Do unto others as you would have them do unto you." If that is one's code of behavior, in my opinion, that person is moral. That is my code.

Texas is more than a place. It is a frame of mind. A Texan believes that the individual is powerful. Texas has that rugged individualism. It may not be polished, may not be smooth, and it may not be silky, but it is there. I believe that I get from the soil and the spirit of Texas the feeling that I, as an individual, can accomplish whatever I want to and that there are no limits, that you can just keep going, just keep soaring. I like that spirit.

When Barbara Jordan was elected to the Texas Senate in 1966, she became the first black senator to sit in that body since 1883. She was elected to the United States House of Representatives in 1972 and served for three highly visible terms. In 1979, she became a professor at the Lyndon Baines Johnson School of Public Affairs at the University of Texas in Austin.

Toni Morrison

Born February 18, 1931, in Lorain, Ohio

Toni Morrison is one of America's most celebrated and successful novelists. In 1993, her magical use of words captured the Nobel Prize for Literature. She was the eighth woman and the first African American woman to be so recognized. The author of eight books, Paradise, *published in 1997, is her most recent novel. She was awarded the Pulitzer Prize for Fiction in 1988 for her fifth novel,* Beloved, *and received the National Book Critics Award for* Song of Solomon *in 1978. She was the Albert Schweitzer Professor of Humanities at the State University of New York at Albany before assuming the Robert Goheen Professorship in the Humanities Council at Princeton University in 1989.*

I remember myself as surrounded by extraordinary adults who were smarter than me. I was better educated, but I always thought that they had true wisdom and I had merely book learning. It was only when I began to write that I was able to marry those two things: wisdom and education.

Being a black woman novelist is a novel position. When I turned in the manuscript of *The Bluest Eye* in 1968, there was a lot of interest in certain kinds of black expression. But I had written something separate from the harangue and the confusion. The company that published my first book didn't have any sense of my being a person who could write a second one. They weren't buying a writer, they were buying that one book because it was black—not because they thought it was any good.

You can't evolve good criticism until you have good books. I was in publishing and felt that white editors didn't always give black writers the respect of serious and rigorous editing that they deserved. And it was hard to get the balanced attention of the critics and reviewers because they wanted to talk about anything but political implications. Then they started talking about the political implications and they never talked about the artistic strategies. They didn't give you two legs to walk on, always one.

Now the reading of black fiction is becoming systematically analyzed. There is the emergence of theories of criticism that address the art and its culture.

If you're going to hold someone down you're going to have to hold onto the other end of the chain. You are confined by your own system of repression.

My job is to not become anybody's creature, not the publisher's, not the critical establishment's, not the media's, not anybody's. I'm not doing anyone justice, not the women's movement, not the black movement, not novels, not anyone, if I toe the line. I want to write better. Think better. I don't know how not to want that. And better for me may not be in step with what is current and prevailing.

When I first began to write, I was a little breathless, because I wasn't sure that a particular expression or sensibility would be there tomorrow. And one can panic under those circumstances. Then you learn that, yes, you may forget the perfect sentence you thought of in a traffic jam, it may not come back. And then you realize it doesn't matter because a better one will come.

I never played it safe in a book. I never tried to play to the gallery. For me, it was this extraordinary exploration. You have to be willing to think the unthinkable.

I always think I'm at some archaeological site and I find this shard, a little piece of pottery and then I have to invent the rest. But first I have to go to the place, move the dirt, find why I am there. What's interesting here, why are you frightened, what is it that keeps nagging you? Then you see something, it may be a color, an image, a voice, and you build from it.

When the Pulitzer was awarded, the response in many quarters—white, black, male, female, young and old—was "we." "We did it!" It had a sense of hallelujah about it. But it's foolish to surrender to that because it interferes with work. I'd begin to think of myself in my sleep as Toni Morrison comma Pulitzer Prize, and never get anything done.

Writing wonderful books is not going to make me a wonderful person. I alone can improve myself and make myself more like the person I would like to grow to be.

I hate ideological whiteness. I hate when people come into my presence and become white. I'd just been elected to the American Academy of Arts and Letters and a man whom I used to read in anthologies came up to me and said, "Hello, welcome to the Academy." Then his third sentence was about his splendid black housekeeper. This little code saying, "I like black people or I know one," is humiliating for me—and should have been for him.

In the beginning, people asked me a lot of questions about whether I consider myself a black writer or a woman writer. I was fighting shy of labels that had quite other meanings. Obviously, any artist wants to feel that there is something in her work that all peoples of the world are receptive to. On the other hand, I did not want to be erased. I didn't want my blackness to be erased, I didn't want my femininity to be erased. I wanted it to be very clear that "universal" is not for me a buzzword for not political or not ethnic.

Althea T. L. Simmons

Born April 17, 1924, in Shreveport, Louisiana
Died September 13, 1990, in Washington, D.C.

A turning point in my life came while I was at Southern University. Thurgood Marshall came to Louisiana to argue the equalization of teachers' salaries. He asked to have two students take notes and, luckily, I was one of them. I saw him question the state superintendent of education who squirmed like a little boy who had gotten caught with his hand in the cookie jar. I said wherever Marshall went to law school that's where I wanted to go. I went to Howard University because that's where they were teaching civil rights.

When I got out of law school in 1956, I went back home to Dallas and the person I was working for was the dean of black lawyers in Texas. He said, "All right, baby, I'm going to teach you some law." The first case I had to do some research on was the State of Texas against the NAACP. They were putting the NAACP out of business.

After being a volunteer for the NAACP, I decided to come on staff for one year to help them out. Well, that one year was over twenty-five years ago.

When Clarence Mitchell, who was my predecessor in this job and who had been here twenty-nine years, retired in 1978, I was transferred to Washington to be the chief lobbyist. Clarence Mitchell was a living legend. There was not a civil rights measure that had been passed in modern history that his fingerprints were not on.

I recall quite vividly when Mr. [Benjamin] Hooks [Executive Director of the NAACP] took me to the White House to introduce me to President Carter. The President said, "Miss Simmons, you've got some very big shoes to fill." And I said, respectfully, "Mr. President, nobody can fill Clarence Mitchell's shoes. I'll have to walk in my own footsteps."

I think I have the respect of both parties on the Hill. A lobbyist's stock in trade is your credibility, and even though I had my association, whether or not I could represent it depended on me.

I often say that I am a double minority, black and female, and it cuts both ways. Even when I'm accepted as a black, I have to fight the female portion. If you're female, you've got to be able to prove that once a month you're not going to go down the drain, that you're able to hold your own. And that's true within the race and outside the race.

We do the voting records on all 535 members of the Congress. We put out voting records on a quarterly basis and then we do what we call a civil rights report card. When a bill is signed into law, it gives me a good feeling to know that I was here and an important link in the chain that made this law a reality.

You find people who misunderstand affirmative action. We still have not determined that America is for everybody. If you go to Appalachia with rural whites, you can really see it when you start talking about empowerment. When you find people in certain classes, there is an attempt to keep them in those classes, be it the rural white in Appalachia or the rural black.

When the 1964 Civil Rights Act passed with the public accommodations section, we went down to Mississippi to help people learn to use the law. I stayed in a motel where the windows went all the way down to the floor, and I was terrified. I put a chair on the bed next to the window, then my luggage and then another chair. Then I got on the edge of that other bed and had one hand on the floor and one hip on the bed. That's how I slept. But we knew that if some of us didn't go down there and stay in those motels and go to those eating places, the folk who *were* there would be loath to go because of the hostility. The Congress had spoken, the President had signed the bill, and we had to show that it was available for them.

In Mississippi two young Klansmen came in and threw trash on the table where my secretary was registering people to vote. They said to get out of town and that they were going to tear the place up. I walked up to one of them and jammed my finger in his chest and said, "You don't tear up anything I put together. Now get out of here!" Common sense would tell you, don't do that. I didn't think, I just acted. I was mad.

The most dehumanizing incident of my life occurred in the late 1950s while we were trying to desegregate the eating facilities in Dallas. My sister, who was one of the first black students in law school at SMU [Southern Methodist University], and a white male law student and I sat at the lunch counter in the bus station downtown. Nobody shouted at us, nobody said anything to us, nobody wiped the counter where we were. They just ignored us. We sat there for about five or six hours. Nobody made any kind of gesture that could be perceived as being hostile. We just didn't exist. Even now it's painful because I am a person and for all practical purposes, I did not exist.

We are seeing increased racial bigotry and that disturbs me. There should be no need for my organization. We're trying to work ourselves out of business. Unfortunately, I wanted to see that in my lifetime.

Have I given up hope? No. I am an incurable activist. I can't believe that the American people are so closed-minded that they can't see the necessity to use all our human resources.

Althea Simmons was the chief congressional lobbyist of the National Association for the Advancement of Colored People and the director of the civil rights organization's Washington bureau. She came to Washington after two decades of field experience and administrative positions with the NAACP. Considered one of the most effective lobbyists on Capitol Hill, she played a key role in such legislative victories as the 1982 extension of the Voting Rights Act, sanctions against South Africa, and a national holiday honoring Dr. Martin Luther King, Jr.

Maxine Waters

Born August 15, 1938, in St. Louis, Missouri

Maxine Waters came to Washington in 1991 from the California State Assembly with 78 percent of the vote. She rose to national prominence a year later during the 1992 Los Angeles rebellion. Among her notable legislative efforts is a $50 million appropriation bill for her "Youth Fair Chance" program, which trains unskilled, unemployed people nationwide. In 1997, she was elected Chairperson of the Congressional Black Caucus, and she is a member of the House Judiciary Committee. Waters was elected to the California State Assembly in 1976, where she worked on a wide range of legislation, from sex abuse prevention to corporate divestment from South Africa.

When you have twelve sisters and brothers, and you are competing for everything from space in the bathroom to the most favorable bed, I suppose it helps to shape the personality an awful lot.

For the most part we were raised on welfare. I can remember the visits from the social worker, who, in my estimation, was a very important person. Not only was the social worker someone who was dressed nicely, with a briefcase, who came to your house, she appeared to have a lot of power. That's what I wanted to be, a very important social worker.

As just a little girl, I always managed to get in control of whatever the situation was. We used to have bill collectors come by our house to collect on the fifteen-cent insurance policies, or the furniture store would send its guy by to collect, and I disliked it an awful lot. Many of them did not treat your house with respect. They would walk in without knocking. At one point, I said to my mother, "Let me go pay the bills for you." I would run around and pay these bills. That was kind of powerful, I felt a sense of responsibility in doing that.

One of the things I considered a delightful experience in school was the Constitution and the Bill of Rights. I didn't realize the gap was so big from the Founding Fathers until now. And I didn't realize they weren't talking about me.

Poor people have not ever really organized to use their numbers and their powers to force governments to do very much for them. People who don't make a lot of noise don't get very much. All of those twelve sisters and brothers and little kids, whether they are in Saint Louis or Watts or the Bronx or Harlem or Appalachia, deserve to have the system work for them. This system does not simply belong to the people who have money and power.

If you take a look at poor communities all over the country, you will find that many of us emerged into leadership roles through heading poverty program organizations.

When I came to this legislature, I did things my own way because I really didn't have any guidepost. Even if I had been a willing pupil, there were no teachers for women here.

One of the greatest things about this job is that it's a platform, a forum to raise issues and discuss things that, perhaps, nobody else would discuss if you were not here. I'm convinced that South Africa would not have been on this agenda, and divestment never would have occurred, if I had not been here. We'd never have been able to pass it into law if I hadn't acted on instinct one day when I saw an opportunity to leverage something that the governor and everybody else wanted. I'm proud of that.

In all of my young years, I lived in a society that discriminated against me and my family and my neighbors and my friends. And we were confined to this ghetto. We just didn't know a lot about what was going on out there in the world and what we had a right to participate in.

One of the things developed in the Head Start program was taking children on trips. The average Head Start child never moved more than a few miles beyond where they lived. The housing projects have become the world for many of those children. They are isolated and cut off in that world. You can see all of the anger and frustration. They know something is wrong.

Head Start was an extremely important turning point in my life. It was to help families take control of their children's educational destiny. I came to understand that it was important to me to pursue those things that I cared about, and I really didn't care if people didn't like me for it. It's fine if you can get along with people. And, yes, we live in a society where some diplomacy makes good sense. But in the final analysis, you must not give up your beliefs in order to simply have people like you.

I like to laugh, I like to have a great time. But I also have a right to my anger, and I don't want anybody telling me I shouldn't be, that it's not nice to be, and that something's wrong with me because I get angry.

Black women are going to have to take more leadership. I think we are prepared because we bring a tenaciousness with us. We do not fear losing friends, allies, or jobs.

Older black women have always been so helpful. I think that if the world is ever going to be changed, that's who's going to really do it.

I wasn't in the cotton fields, but I've been on a job where I was working in a factory, and I had two little kids and I didn't have much money. And sometimes I had to walk from the factory downtown, home. I had older women who not only kept my children for me but also cooked dinner so I could eat. That wasn't their job. I didn't pay them for it. I could barely pay them to keep the kids. How could you not love that?

I collect black memorabilia and I love Aunt Jemima. I do. No matter how they try to depict her as being fat, black, and ugly, with big lips and all of that, she symbolizes for me what has held us in good stead all of these years.

Johnnetta Betsch Cole

Born October 19, 1936, in Jacksonville, Florida

Dr. Johnetta Cole was the first black woman to serve as president of Spellman College. She retired from the position in 1997, and joined Atlanta's Emory University as Presidential Distinguished Professor in 1998. In 1992, Dr. Cole served as member of President-elect Clinton's transition team as Cluster Coordinator for Education, Labor, and the Arts and Humanities. All American Women *and* Anthropology for the Nineties, *textbooks edited by Dr. Cole, are used in college classrooms across America. She is the author of* Conversations: Straight Talk with America's Sister President, *published in 1993. Her latest book is* Dream the Boldest Dreams: And Other Lessons of Life, *published in 1997.*

I grew up in a middle, upper-middle-class family. My great-grandfather was the founder of the first insurance company in the state of Florida. We lived in this wonderful house, which sat in a wonderful location facing a gorgeous park. Idyllic stuff—palm trees, swimming pool, and swings. With one problem. That pool was for white folks only and those swings were not for me.

How do you explain that to a kid without creating the kind of anger and hostility which could boomerang? How do you do that without challenging the existence of a God, of a moral system, of a democratic process? I think one of the most extraordinary untold stories is the story of black parenting. What do you tell your kid—"Don't worry, it'll go away quickly"?

When we talk about feelings of solidarity, of kinship, of sisterhood, I think what we're really talking about is shared experiences. . . .

Everybody knows about "the kitchen" because when we were little girls sitting between those knees that served like locks, when they came with that brush or comb, you got ready because they would inevitably get to "the kitchen," the nape of the neck, and you knew it was going to hurt.

But why call it "the kitchen"? Why not call it "the pantry"? I think, because the kitchen has been the most difficult place for us all our lives. When black women came home to their own kitchen after working in Miss Ann's, there was that inevitable double shift. When the black man came home, there was the notion that he ought to rest. The sister went to the kitchen to start again.

If we think that our daughters ought not to have to come home from a job and exclusively be the ones to do the second shift, washing the dishes, changing the clothes, and cleaning the house, then we'd better tell our sons that now. And they'd better learn to do that now. And if we think that our daughters ought to be in Congress next to our sons, we'd better let our sons know that now, so they get prepared to have women as colleagues.

Black women ain't been put on no pedestals. Nine out of every ten black women worked in the fields alongside black men. But every time we have this image of slavery, there she is, either setting the table for master or getting in his bed. This myth of black women profiting at the expense of black men is the oldest rap around. It's been unbelievably important to keep it going, to divide black men from black women. I spent two years in Liberia during the sixties. There I was in a country for the first time in my life where I was in the majority, a land of black folk. And it was important that I saw inequality. It was important to see descendants of slaves who came to the U.S. and in the late 1840s went back to Liberia, to see them being Mr. Charlie and Miss Ann to those black folk who—what?—didn't have the privilege of coming to America as slaves? That relationship of inequality was not color-coded.

I had a friend who also served as my interpreter who taught me, very vividly, the power of language. If he wanted something from me he would call me "Mother," and he would use the Kissi word. If he was absolutely disgusted because for the ninety-ninth time I had made some *faux pas* culturally, he would just look at me, suck his teeth, and say, "My child." But there was a third way that sent chills through my body and he knew it. When he was angry he would call me "Missy." He was saying, you are acting like a white American woman.

If folk can learn to be racist, then they can learn to be antiracist. If being a sexist ain't genetic, then, dad gum, people can learn about gender equality.

I learned how to be the president of this college by watching black women more than by reading some manual.

I like the notion of being an intellectual, but there are all these women who were not an Ida B. Wells or Anna J. Cooper, but who were nevertheless intellectuals, political and academic leaders. What else can you call somebody who takes scruffy kids off the streets into the colored branch of the library and helps them love ideas? That's an intellectual.

At the same time that I want this image of "sheroes," black sheroes, we've got to be careful, because if we focus too much on all of those who have made it, then we forget those who never could.

Black women who were in the day-to-day struggle learned that we were to take the notes and not chair the meetings, that we were to form the picket lines but not speak to the press. It's a bitter experience when the assumption is that it's for all of us, and then you find out it's for some of us. It's been a bitter experience for millions of black women who assumed that the women's movement was for all of us and then we found out, one more time, for some of us. . . .

Where are the women in black studies? Where are the black folks in women's studies? Black women get shut out of both.

Systems of inequality tell you what you can and cannot do. Elaborate structures have to be built to convince you, because you know you can do it. You just did it.

Norma Merrick Sklarek

Born April 15, 1928, in New York City, New York

Norma Sklarek was the first black woman to become a licensed architect in the states of New York and California—indeed, in the entire United States. She was also the first black woman to be honored by fellowship in the American Institute of Architects (AIA). Projects to her credit include the San Bernardino (California) City Hall, the United States Embassy in Tokyo, and Terminal One at Los Angeles International Airport. Ms. Sklarek retired from the firm of Jon Jerde, Inc. in 1995, and works as a consultant to other architects. Howard University has named an award in her honor, to be presented annually to an architectural student of special merit.

I had never seen a T-square or a triangle before I entered the School of Architecture at Columbia University. I found throughout my experiences that if something is very tough initially, after I work at it, I not only catch up but move on ahead.

I always knew that I was going to have a profession in order to work, that nobody was going to be taking care of me. All of my contemporaries, black girls, knew that they were going to have to work and that they would work for their entire lifetime.

I graduated from school in 1950. Until the end of World War II, I think there was strong discrimination against women in architecture. The schools had a quota, it was obvious, a quota against women and a quota against blacks.

In architecture, I had absolutely no role model. I'm happy today to be a role model for others that follow.

Even after graduation from school, it was tough for women to get a job. I went to about twenty different offices before I was able to get a job. And there were things that I didn't like when I first started working, like not being able to get meaningful assignments. There's a difference between ten years of experience and one year of experience repeated ten times.

After World War II, building increased exponentially and they started building offices. They were hiring more women and people from other countries. I got a job in 1955 with one of the largest and most prestigious architectural firms in the United States, Skidmore, Owings & Merrill. I did all of the complicated detailing on major projects. I was at Gruen Associates for twenty years, about seventeen of those as head of the architectural department. I was the first woman vice-president at Welton, Becket, and I got the assignment of L.A.X. Terminal One.

I was keenly aware from the time I first started that I was highly visible in an office where there are a hundred people and nearly all of them are white males, and that I'm black and female. I stand out.

When I first moved to California, I didn't have a car immediately, and a co-worker who lived nearby offered to drive me to work. He was late every morning. It only took about one week for the boss to tell me, inform me, what the office hours were, because every day we were fifteen to twenty minutes late. He hadn't noticed that this joker I was riding with had been late for two years.

If you're late ten minutes or so, it's going to be noticed. But if you produce more work and you're early, that's also noticed.

In order to call yourself an architect, one should be licensed in one of the states. There are very few black women still that are licensed. I became licensed in California in 1962, and it wasn't until about twenty years later that the second black woman became licensed. I don't think there are more than twelve in the entire United States at this time.

Siegel-Sklarek-Diamond is unique in that we are probably the largest totally woman-owned architectural firm in the United States. Most of the employees are young women and the reason is that they feel more comfortable with us. They apply in far greater numbers. They know that they have not been given a fair break in other offices where guys with lesser qualifications were given more challenging assignments.

I was the first woman, and still the only one, in the ninety-year history of the Los Angeles chapter to receive fellowship with the AIA. At the time I worked for a large firm, and even though I had that kind of honor and recognition, I still was not a partner at that firm.

I only have one lifetime and I would like to see more progress in my lifetime. Many of the younger generation think of the more serious problems in civil rights as being a hundred years ago, not being thirty or twenty years ago.

Construction and architecture have traditionally been a male bastion and they perceive architects—not only architects but those in power in any field—as being males.

Projects don't just come to us. Most of our projects are not in the public sector, government projects. Even though there is an affirmative-action policy with government work, we still have to do an enormous marketing job and spend an awful lot of money in order to get it, to prove that we're not just equal to, but better than any of the male firms.

We're working on some low-cost housing and it's very difficult to do anything really good with their criteria. You're not allowed to do things which would improve the quality of life in the building. For example, we wanted to offset the units on the ground floor to provide a space that a tenant could feel was his or her own. The clients know that every corner costs two dollars more, but we're not permitted to do anything like that, even though we could bring the total within a certain budget. Which means you've got them all in a straight line.

Architecture should be working on improving the environment of people in their homes, in their places of work, and their places of recreation. It should be functional and pleasant, not just in the image of the architect's ego.

Gwendolyn Brooks

Born June 7, 1917, in Topeka, Kansas

My first four poems were published at the age of eleven. When I was fifteen, I began writing to people like James Weldon Johnson. He was very kind and sent back my manuscripts with marginal notes, little assistances. He thought I was talented and hoped that I would keep writing. My parents were delighted with all of this attention. There was an enthusiasm that meant so much. But I would have gone on writing. I didn't care what any of them said.

In writing poetry you're interested in condensation so you don't try to put all of a particular impression or inspiration on a single page. You distill. Poetry is life distilled.

I have written poems about my response to some of the things that were happening. When Emmett Till was murdered, I couldn't have any rest until I wrote about that. I couldn't rest until I had done something, done my kind of something, because my own son was fourteen at the same time Emmett Till was murdered at the age of fourteen.

Much of *Maud Martha* is autobiographical. I didn't want to write about somebody who turned out to be a star 'cause most people don't turn out to be stars. And yet their lives are just as sweet and just as rich as any others and often they are richer and sweeter.

My poem, "Ballad of Pearl May Lee," examines the whole thing from the viewpoint of the dark-complexioned black woman. It expresses the way a lot of women of my complexion feel. They have been neglected in favor of light-complexioned black women.

When I read it on the campus of the University of California at Berkeley, a young black fellow in the audience said, "I hear you, Sister." I love that. "I hear you, Sister."

I have to come to that paper excited. They always say, "You read your poem so beautifully. How does that happen?" I say, "When you're writing a poem, you're not sitting there all cold and dull and dim. You're all excited." I try to read poetry to give an impression of how I felt when I was writing it.

"It is the morning of our love." It seemed like a beautiful, simple way to start a love poem, but it was a mistake. I tell poets that when a line just floats into your head, don't pay attention 'cause it probably has floated into somebody else's head. Sure enough I found it in another poem. So now I don't use that and the poem begins, "In a package of minutes, there is this 'we,' " which is a line I struggled over. So I don't expect to see it anywhere.

I can't think of any time that I would choose to have grown up in rather than this time. Fascinating things have happened, would-be revolutions of various kinds.

There was a gang in Chicago called the Blackstone Rangers. About five thousand young blacks were in it. So powerful were they that in 1967 when a television station wanted to come into the neighborhood and make a documentary on my life, we had to get permission from the Blackstone Rangers. I started a workshop for those who were interested in writing.

The young people that I met in the late sixties—when resentment was reasonable—educated me. They gave me books to read. We talked and talked. They just absorbed me, adopted me. We went lots of places together.

We would just walk into a tavern and [poet] Haki Madhubuti would say, "Look, folks, we're gonna lay some poetry on you." And he would recite a poem. And if I could read a poem like "We real cool," very short, I could avoid having drinks thrown at me. I mean, that's enlarging a point a bit, but after all, these people were not there to listen to poetry.

I go to lots of prisons to recite poetry. What I usually do now is have the prisoners read also. They always have manuscripts. There's anger and there's a lot of love poetry being written and there's a sensitivity to what's going on politically.

I'm writing a book about Winnie Mandela. Most of my friends are against us going to South Africa. I have no intention of going to South Africa ever to be an honorary white.

There are so many blacks who are denying all blackness. They think they can twinkle their fingers at blackness and it'll just go away and they'll be loved by whites and accepted.

When I meet these young people who talk about being raised in white neighborhoods, who've seen virtually no blacks and don't want to see any, I just encourage them to keep talking because strange things begin to come out, one of which is this yearning toward black validation.

Malcolm X, who said he was not going to turn the other cheek, expressed the kind of sentiments I hold with. Here was a man—big, strong, courageous. And he wasn't endlessly pushing to integrate with whites. He believed black people should love black people and value them above all others.

I don't like the idea of the black race being diluted out of existence. I like the idea of all of us being here.

Gwendolyn Brooks won the Pulitzer Prize for Poetry in 1950 for her book, Annie Allen. *She was the first black writer to win the prestigious award. Considered "the Bard of Bronzeville," she was also poet laureate of Illinois for sixteen years and poetry consultant to the Library of Congress. Her most recent book of poetry,* Children Coming Home, *was published in 1991. Her autobiography,* Report from Part One, *was published in 1973; the second installment,* Report from Part Two, *was published in 1996. The Gwendolyn Brooks Center for Black Literature and Culture, where she is Writer-In-Residence, was dedicated at Chicago State University in 1993.*

Leontyne Price

Born February 10, 1927, in Laurel, Mississippi

When Leontyne Price debuted at the Metropolitan Opera House in 1961, she received a rapturous forty-two-minute ovation for her performance as Leonora in Il Trovatore. *The seventh black person to make a Metropolitan debut, she was the first to achieve worldwide status as* prima donna assoluta. *Her retelling of Verdi's* Aida *as a story for children, entitled* Aida Told by Leontyne Price, *was published in 1990. Ms. Price remains the most honored of her generation of singers, with awards that include eighteen Grammy awards and the Presidential Medal of Freedom. Most recently, she received the prestigious Meadows Award from Southern Methodist University and the Meadows Foundation in Dallas, Texas.*

My mother is responsible for having delivered more babies than any midwife in the history of Jones County, Mississippi. To this date, she is my greatest inspiration.

The way I was taught, being black was a plus, always. Being a human being, being in America, and being black, all three were the greatest things that could happen to you. The combination was unbeatable.

I received a toy piano for Christmas at the age of five or six. I had an awful lot of attention, I was center stage from the time I received that toy piano. I felt a musical sense of direction. I had the disease then, I could tell, because you really have to be a monster very early.

I think we performers are monsters. We are a totally different, far-out race of people. I totally and completely admit, with no qualms at all, my egomania, my selfishness, coupled with a really magnificent voice.

In some of my operatic roles—maybe the strength of my portrayal of Aida—I reveal the wonderful thing that it is to be a black princess.

My mother took me to see Marian Anderson. When I saw this wonderful woman come from the wings in this white satin dress, I knew instantly: one of these days, I'm going to come out of the wings. I don't know what color the dress is going to be but I'm going to be center stage, right there, where I saw her. The light dawned. It was a magic moment.

My proudest moment, operatically speaking, was my debut at the Metropolitan. It was my first real victory, my first unqualified acceptance as an American, as a human being, as a black, as an artist, the whole thing.

I was the first black diva that was going to hang on. My being prepared is the reason I didn't go away. That is really the substance of my pioneering. Marian [Anderson] had opened the door. I kept it from closing again.

I sang seven roles my first season at the Metropolitan Opera, I was that prepared. My first invitation to the Metropolitan I refused, because I was not.

Art is the only thing you cannot punch a button for. You must do it the old-fashioned way. Stay up and really burn the midnight oil. There are no compromises.

Accomplishments have no color.

The Prices and the Chisolms have been friends all our lives. Those two families helped to bridge the gap in Laurel. My aunt was in the Chisolms' domestic service for fifty years. My parents were married on their estate. After I graduated with a teacher's degree from Central State College in Ohio, they were my sponsors for my New York studies at Juilliard.

Nobody ever thought of a career, nobody had that much money to gamble on it, which is the reason that some young people even now don't go into the classical field unless they have a sponsor. It's too difficult, too dangerous.

My father never understood it but he thought it was the most glorious thing he had ever heard in his life, that his baby girl would have this ability to understand all this stuff.

I don't love anything more than hearing my own voice. It's a personal adoration.

Listening to my recordings is like filling your pores with inspiration, and where better to get it from than yourself, because that substance is a combination of everyone who contributed something, your mama, your papa, the community, your teachers, everybody and everything. Applause is the fulfillment. From Mississippi to the Met. That's the pinnacle. That forty-two minute ovation was like having climbed the mountain. . . .

Once you get on stage, everything is right. I feel the most beautiful, complete, fulfilled. I think that's why, in the case of noncompromising career women, parts of our personal lives don't work out. One person can't give you the feeling that thousands of people give you.

I have never given all of myself, even vocally, to anyone. I was taught to sing on your interest, not your capital.

I do like being in competition with me.

I never thought any institution was more important than myself. I think that happens, for example, in Hollywood. You let the institution take you over and you are vulnerable, which means that when they get ready, they can discard you.

I wasn't uncomfortable singing at the inaugural ceremony for my friend William Winter, the governor of Mississippi, because I thought I belonged there. It was as much my capital as his.

We should not have a tin cup out for something as important as the arts in this country, the richest in the world. Creative artists are always begging, but always being used when it's time to show us at our best.

You should always know when you're shifting gears in life. You should leave your era, it should never leave you.

Now I'm doing recitals, orchestra things, master classes. If somebody thinks I can still sing, I've got a wheelchair in the wings. But I have not retired. From pressure I have retired, but I'm not ever going to retire from anything else.

Althea Gibson

Born August 25, 1927, in Silver, South Carolina

When I was younger I just stayed away from home. All I did was maybe ride the subways back and forth and walk various sections of New York. They called me a wayward child. When I did come home, I knew what to expect when my father came home. Not a spankin', a whippin'.

My parents were doing their best to raise me, but I just didn't let 'em. When I was given a ticker-tape parade after winning Wimbledon in fifty-seven, you could see no prouder parents of any child in life than my mother and father.

I learned paddle tennis with a friend of mine on 143rd Street. She and I were competitors. The young boys who played on another court up the block heard about me and challenged me. And I accepted. I played it all—basketball, shuffleboard, badminton, volleyball. I just loved to play.

Buddy Walker was the first to help me. After seeing me play paddle tennis in forty-two or forty-three, he gave me my first tennis racket and introduced me to the Cosmopolitan Tennis Club up on Convent Avenue. The teaching pro at the club was Fred Johnson. He lost his left arm in the war, and believe it or not, he was the one who taught me the service toss and racket preparation. With one arm.

I played and practiced most of my life in Harlem on boards, on wood. Fastest court surface in the world. Balls come at you like bullets. That helped me when I played on other fast surfaces like grass at Wimbledon.

I knew that I was an unusual, talented girl through the grace of God. I didn't need to prove that to myself. I only wanted to prove it to my opponents.

I first played at Wimbledon in 1951. My very first match was scheduled for the famed Centre Court. I made a vow to myself: Althea, you're not going to look around. You're not going to listen to any calls or remarks. All you are going to do is watch the tennis ball. I did that. I didn't acknowledge the referees' calls; whatever they said, okay fine. I won the first set six–love. Then I looked around at the nineteen- to twenty-thousand spectators as if to say, "How do you like that?" But then after that I lost the second set six–love because I lost my concentration.

After being the black champion of the American Tennis Association for ten consecutive years I felt I was ready. After fifty-six nobody could beat me. . . .

I had the best serve in women's tennis. I had the best overhead in women's tennis. And I had the most killing volley in women's tennis.

You got to know your opponent. You got to know their strengths, their weaknesses, see how they move, what balls they don't like. Once I know this, they only see the ball at their weak points, not their strengths.

I was ruthless on the tennis court. Win at any cost. I became an attacker. If your first serve ain't good, I'll knock it down your throat. It just so happened that I had the talent to win at another level instead of being the meanie on the tennis court.

Before the singles finals at Wimbledon they came into the locker room to show us how to curtsy to the Queen when we were introduced on Centre Court—which I did, I thought, very gracefully. Upon winning the championship, she came down on Centre Court to present me with the trophy. That was quite an honor.

Althea Gibson was the first black American to play tennis at the U.S. Open (1950) and Wimbeldon, England (1951). With her triumph in the women's singles and doubles at the prestigious English tournament in 1957, she became the first black tennis player to win that championship. Later that year she added the U.S. women's singles title at Forest Hills, and in 1958 she repeated the same round of victories. Her autobiography, I Always Wanted to Be Somebody, *was published in 1958. She joined the Ladies' Professional Golf Association in 1963 and, in 1988, she was appointed special consultant to the New Jersey Governor's Council of Physical Fitness in Sports.*

Ernestine Anderson

Born November 11, 1928, in Houston, Texas

A precocious talent for jazz led Ernestine Anderson to sing and tour with big bands of the 1940s and 1950s, including those of Johnny Otis, Russell Jacquet, and Lionel Hampton. Like her surprising image, her brand of music-making these days is infused with more than the Blues. After singing the music of others for more than fifty years, Ernestine Anderson is writing songs of her own. She made her songwriting debut on her acclaimed album Now and Then, *released in 1993, and more Anderson tunes are featured on the 1996 follow-up,* Blues, Dues and Love News. *Her latest collection,* Isn't It Romantic, *was released in 1998.*

I came home one day after I got beat up by these kids saying how I hated white people. And my grandmother had this swing on her porch as many people do in the South. And whenever I had a problem, I would always go to my grandmother, and somehow the problem would get solved. She would get her favorite pop, which was cream soda, and mine too, and we'd sit in the swing. And there was something about sitting in this swing and swinging back and forth, that just sort of calmed me down, with her talking to me. So I came home in a rage this time, saying, "I hate 'em, I hate 'em." And she sat there and started swinging me back and forth until I calmed down, and then she said, in a very soothing voice, "Before you go to bed tonight, I want you to say a prayer for those people." I loved my grandmother so much, but I found myself saying, "Mama, I can't do it." And she said, "Well, you have to, because you cannot carry hate in your heart for anybody, for any man." She said, "You're a young person, and one day you'll move away from Texas, and you'll find that all people are not like these people here." I thought about it, through several bottles of soda. And finally, she got me to say I would say a prayer before I went to bed.

As a kid I remember sitting at the window pretending the window ledge was a piano. I marked it with pencils in black and white. I'd have the radio on and I'd be singing to the radio and playing that windowsill piano. . . .

The Eldorado Ballroom—this was back in Houston and I was twelve years old—had an amateur contest going. The piano player asked me what key did I do. At that time I knew only two pop songs. I said C. It turned out to be the wrong key. But my grandmother had been coaxing me and telling me that if you want to be a professional, once you start singing, just keep on going. Anyway, I started singing and I improvised around the melody. When I finished, one of the musicians in the band told me I was a jazz singer. So that was my introduction to jazz.

When I was in junior high school I was working one night a week as a singer. I would do my two songs and people would throw money—paper dollars and silver dollars—up on the stage. So much money that they had these two guys with long brooms sweeping it up into piles. It was a bunch of money. And I also got paid—twenty-five dollars or something like that—and all the soda pop I could drink.

My dad had been working on a job in Houston for a number of years. They hired this white guy who was there just one day when he said, "Before I hand a tool to a nigger, I'll quit." They fired my dad. It tore him apart. So that's me, that's a part of me.

For many, many years, I hated the blues. My parents used to play the blues all the time. And then, years later on down the line, the blues sounded and felt good to me. And I think it was because by then I had lived the blues, and I think that's what you have to do. Nobody can teach you how to sing the blues, you have to feel the blues.

I learned how to listen to other singers and take from them certain things and still have my own identity. Everybody is influenced by somebody or something. If there's an original, who is the original?

These influences are still in my life. Sarah Vaughan, for her breath control and just being able to do whatever she wants to do with her voice, her total control. Ella Fitzgerald, for her clarity and just swinging you into bad health. She becomes an instrument. And Sarah's phrasing, her choice of notes—she dares to be daring.

I don't think jazz ever died. It suffered a setback during the sixties. I had to move to London in order to work because a jazz person couldn't get work in the United States when rock 'n' roll became the music. I didn't think it would last this long, and I don't think the rock 'n' roll people thought it would last this long, but it has.

The low had to be in the late sixties when my depression reached its peak. When I moved back to Seattle from London, it was like starting all over again and I just couldn't imagine going through that struggle, paying dues all over again. Also I was missing my children. It hurt because I felt I was sacrificing their growing up for something I wanted so bad, and that was singing. And maybe it was the wrong thing, because I hadn't been successful at it.

I worked as a maid in a motel for two and a half days. I went from there to an answering-service job. They put me on a switchboard that had a lot of entertainers on it. I started getting these feelings that I didn't want to be taking their calls. I wanted to be working, singing again. And so I started chanting.

I was always looking outside myself for strength and confidence. I thought if I had a hit record, I would be happy. I got a hit album in the fifties. I was never so unhappy. A husband, I was unhappy. Freedom, I was really unhappy. A new car, a friend. You stop looking outside yourself for something. This is what Buddhism teaches you. It comes from within. It was there all the time.

Unita Blackwell

Born March 18, 1933, in Lula, Mississippi

The first black woman mayor in Mississippi, Unita Blackwell was elected mayor of Mayersville in 1976. She is chair of the Black Women Mayors' Caucus and second vice-president of the National Conference of Black Mayors. In 1991, she was a TOP Fellow at Harvard University's Institute of Politics at the John F. Kennedy School of Politics. In 1993, she was appointed to serve as chair of the Southern Institute on Children and Families, a position she still holds. In 1997, she was elected Mayor of Mayersville for a fifth four-year term. Mayor Blackwell received the John F. Kennedy Profiles in Courage Award in 1990, and was given a $350,000 MacArthur "Genius" Award in 1992. But for all the degrees and symbols denoting her distinguished achievements, Mississippi's first black woman mayor has never forgotten that prior to 1954, she was a field worker, picking cotton for three dollars a day. It's still listed on her resume.

This very place where I am now the mayor, the people used to arrest me every day and harass me every day. They turned cars upside down, burned crosses in my yard, threw homemade bombs at us.

It wasn't just a song for us, "We Shall Overcome." It was our strength. When I see people heading up organizations and doing all these things, it didn't come about overnight and it didn't come without pain.

I think that a lot of people might have missed the emotional violence, looking at the physical violence during the civil rights movement. The emotional violence was fear and not knowing what's going to happen and when they were coming at you. I experienced the emotional violence every day.

I was involved in the voter registration drives, trying to get people down to the courthouse. If you did that, you took your own life in hand. You knew that you might die or if you happened to live that you would be beaten like Fannie Lou Hamer was beaten, till her body was just hard as a rock.

We wanted to bring people out of the bondage that they were under, the feeling that they were hopeless and helpless. And that was not as easy as said, when the courthouse was surrounded with pickup trucks, with guns, with white people and anger.

I said, "Nothin' from nothin' leaves nothin'. We don't have nothin', so we ain't losing nothin' and our life don't mean nothin' if we continue this way with no freedom." I was determined to have my rights as a citizen in this United States.

I'm one of the people who has filed a lawsuit against almost every agency and operation of white people in the state of Mississippi. We had to. I drove out of my house and I was arrested every day, during one time, every day straight for thirty days. It may be seventy-five times I've been in jail. They wouldn't tell the black people when we were in jail, because then the Klan could get to us in jail. That's how a lot of people were beaten up and killed.

In 1964 my whole sleep habits changed. I never sleep through the night, because that's when the Klan came at us. We'd take turns, watching, walking, looking. You come talking about you're going to call the police? You couldn't trust nobody because the police was the Klans. The police was burning the cross in my yard.

I called the FBI in Jackson. You can't hold no long conversations with people getting ready to kill you, you see. "Well, how many crosses is it?" he asked. "How tall is the cross?" I wasn't about to get up off the floor to find out how tall the

cross was. And then this FBI man told me how to preserve the cross. Asked me did I have a gunny sack. Gave me a description of what a gunny sack was . . .

Have you ever been in a condition where there is no place you can call for help?

We were denied and disenfranchised in Mississippi, so we formed our own party, the Mississippi Freedom Democratic party. We had sixty-four blacks and four whites to go to Atlantic City.

Mrs. Fannie Lou Hamer testified before the credentials committee. She was my friend and mentor. She helped me understand why white people treated us so bad. She'd say, "Honey, they're just sick, their minds are sick. We're just going to have to get up and get registered to vote so that they can go home and lay down, 'cause they're some sick people." She was the conscience of all of us. She'd have you laughing all the time. In the midst of chaos, we could laugh.

We had no idea that we were changing the whole political future of America. Here was a bunch of people that had never been anywhere, not politically astute people, sophisticated or anything. We were going because we didn't have shoes for our children and decent houses to stay in and just the everyday life that we wanted.

Going to Atlantic City and coming back, we had incidents. When we were coming back, the Klan set up a roadblock. A very petite little woman from Hattiesburg came out with a knife like a razor and laid it around the [white] driver's neck and told him if he stopped she would pull it. We went straight through.

In 1986, we had a convention of the national Conference of Black Mayors in Atlantic City. There we were, black mayors, in limousines and fancy stuff with the police escort in front of us, heading to the place where we were denied the right to be seated twenty some years ago.

I visit countries. I worked on the normalization process between the United States and China as the people-to-people person. I've been to China fifteen times, Hong Kong thirty-six times, I've been to Switzerland, Rumania, India, Central America, and a lot of places. I still come home. I never left Mississippi.

I am the law. I am over the slave owners that used to be over me. I am their mayor. I'm the judge. So it has changed. It's not that subtle thing that we have overcome yet. But that physical outward thing or that mental thing that they're going to get you is not there anymore.

Jewel Plummer Cobb

Born January 17, 1924, in Chicago, Illinois

Dr. Jewel Plummer Cobb is President Emerita of California State University, Fullerton, and has been a Trustee Professor of California State University, Los Angeles since 1990. She earned a Ph.D. in biology from New York University in 1950, and became a prominent cancer researcher specializing in cell biology. She has held several faculty and administrative positions including deanships at Connecticut College and Douglass College at Rutgers University. She was appointed president at Fullerton in 1981. Among her many honors, Dr. Cobb is the recipient of Lifetime Achievement Awards from the National Science Foundation for Contributions to the Advancement of Women and Underrepresented Minorities (1993), and the Kilby Awards Foundation-Southern Methodist University, which honored her in 1995 for Extraordinary Contributions Through Science, Technology, Innovation, Invention, and Education.

When I was a sophomore in high school, I had a microscope given to me in a laboratory to look through, and that was it. I said, "That's for me, biology."

In my family I'm the third-generation doctor. My son, an MD, is the fourth. My father graduated from Cornell in 1908 and from Rush Medical School in Chicago. He was a doctor during the Depression and had his office at the transfer station where black folks came from the stockyards and transferred on the streetcar. So they would come to the office and not have to pay any extra money for transportation.

I first went to the University of Michigan but I left because black students were not allowed to live in the dormitory in 1941. Then I went to a black college and I graduated from Talladega.

After graduate school I did a lot of productive research. I had over thirty-six articles published in basic good stuff in my field, cancer research.

We have a more sophisticated public that will get itself checked more often, but not among the poor. Health care delivery is one of the tragedies still in America. We have not done anything to take care of health care delivery. It's always impacted the poor, but it has now impacted the middle class.

I think of myself as a biologist first—although I'm not doing research now—and an administrator secondly. When I became dean at Connecticut College, I took my research grant and my lab with me [from Sarah Lawrence College] and set up a research lab there, while doing my deaning. I used to go to the lab every morning before I went to my dean's office and a little bit of teaching. I was doing the three things.

I am angry at the condition of society that creates problems for blacks and for women. But I think there are ways anger can be turned into something positive.

The initial shock and nonacceptance and skepticism that existed for me here on my own campus was a "normal American reaction." Because academia is typically white male, [it was] a sexist, racist reaction to a black woman being hired as president. The learning curve, the acceptance curve, is longer and that's how I think racism is manifest.

We have what I would call educational genocide. I'm concerned about learning totally, but I'm immersed in the disastrous record of how many black kids are going into science. They are very few and far between. I've said that when I see more black students in the laboratories than I see on the football field, I'll be happy.

We have a Division 1-A football team with ninety-five members, about 80 percent of whom are black, and about 25 percent of them will graduate. It's very upsetting to me. You know what it's all about: we have resources, we're meat. The solution to the problem is to have a strong academic monitoring program in place. You cannot take tap dancing and flower watching for four years anymore. That's out.

When I retire my plan is to try to work in New York with some kind of systemwide program linking a university with a school system to have what I call Saturday science schools, a whole network of them where youngsters in inner cities can come on Saturdays from nine to twelve o'clock. They would learn more about being comfortable with math and their parents have to be involved. I know that it can work.

We all are aware that America was built on the backs of slaves. There is no debate about that. So I am really p.o.'d about the decimation of the future of the inheritors from this period. The great-grandchildren and great-great-grandchildren of those people that helped found the country are being cast aside and left in the gutters to waste away and then to be blamed. That's what gets to me, blaming the victim.

I hope we can pay teachers the salaries that they deserve. It is absolutely fantastic that we have given such a poor status level to the most important shapers of human character and development we have in this country.

Clara McBride Hale

Born April 1, 1905, in Philadelphia, Pennsylvania
Died December 18, 1992, in New York, New York

My mother always had a house full of children. She had four children and all the neighbors' children came to our house.

You couldn't tell that my mother was not white. See, my grandmother, they said she was a beautiful woman. She was a slave and the master gave her my mother. They had some mulattoes that they called "free issues." That's what happened with my mother. She had all the features of the master and she was as fair.

But she was a fair woman, I mean, not only in color. She knew what was happening and she taught this. She kept saying, "I want you to hold your head up and be proud of yourself. We were brought over and we were enslaved all this time, but it's over now. You're supposed to be free, but you aren't free. Remember that."

My husband and I had dreams of what we were going to do with our children. We dreamed that they'd grow up and be what they want to be and have a good life. My first child was Nathan, Nathan Hale. Oh, I was really an American. I wanted them to know.

My husband died when my daughter Lorraine was five and Nathan was six. There was no way under the sun that they would give you any other job except domestic jobs. And that meant being away all day from these poor little children who had nobody.

So I decided to take in other people's children. They were coming for five days and going home Saturday and Sunday. But they got so they didn't want to go home. They wanted to stay with me altogether. So the parents would give me an extra dollar, and that meant I kept them all the time. My daughter said she was at least eleven years old before she realized that these were not her sisters and brothers.

So I raised forty. Every one of them went to college, every one of them graduated, and they have lovely jobs. They're some of the nicest people. Anything they wanted to do, I backed them up. I have singers, dancers, preachers, and things like that. They're schoolteachers, lawyers, doctors, anything else. No big name or anything, but they're happy.

In 1969, I decided I wouldn't take care of no more children. Then my daughter sent me a girl with an addict baby. Inside of two months I had twenty-two babies living in a five-room apartment. My decision to stop didn't mean anything. It seems as though God wanted them. He kept sending them, and He kept opening a way for me to make it. It's been over six hundred addicted babies.

We hold them and rock them. They love you to tell them how great they are, how good they are. Somehow, even at a young age, they understand that. They're happy and they turn out well.

Being black does not stop you. You can sit out in the world and say, "Well, white people kept me back, and I can't do this." Not so. You can have anything you want if you make up your mind and you want it. You don't have to crack nobody across the head, don't have to steal or anything. Don't have to be smart like the men up high stealing all the money. We're good people and we try.

I'm not going to retire again. Until I die, I'm going to keep doing. My people need me. They need somebody that's not taking from them and is giving them something.

We're going to open a place for children with AIDS because there's no cure and these children will die. People shun them and it's not their fault. I want them to live a good life while they can and know someone loves them.

It's back to being very bad for black people now. But I'll live through that, too. If I don't, I have a daughter that will carry on. I have grandchildren and great-grandchildren. They have the same feeling. When I'm gone, somebody else will take it up and do it. This is how we've lived all these years.

I'm hoping that one day there will be no Hale House, that we won't need anybody to look after these children, that the drugs will be gone.

I'm not an American hero. I'm a person that loves children.

Mother Hale opened the doors of Hale House in a Harlem brownstone in 1973 to provide a life-saving environment for the babies of young drug-addicted mothers. Hundreds of children have returned to health and to their rehabilitated parents after living and being loved in this unique program, which is administered by her daughter, Dr. Lorraine Hale. In 1985, President Ronald Reagan cited Mother Hale as an "American hero."

Ellen Stewart

Born November 7, 1919, in Alexandria, Louisiana

Ellen Stewart is La Mama, the founder and artistic director of La Mama Experimental Theatre Club, an off-off-Broadway theater in New York City. Since its opening in 1961, she has presented more than 1,400 different productions of theater, dance, music, video, and multimedia work. La Mama E.T.C., which often hosts visiting companies, has grown to include three stages, an art gallery, rehearsal studios, and workshop space. In 1985, she received a MacArthur Fellowship, a five-year grant to exceptionally talented and creative people, which she used to begin La Mama Umbria, an artist residence near Spoleto, Italy that is used every summer when the theater in New York is closed. In 1993, Ellen Stewart was inducted into the Broadway Hall of Fame, becoming the first Off-Broadway producer so honored.

I came to New York to study fashion in 1950. I was the first Negro to be called ''Miss'' in Saks Fifth Avenue. Running the elevator at that time was the highest position a colored person could get.

My boss at Saks Fifth Avenue tried to get trained American whites to work with me as the designer and she couldn't get them because whites wouldn't let me be the boss. So who worked with me? I had a department of fifteen people, thirteen of whom were Jewish women, people who had been with top couturiers in their countries and who had managed somehow to survive the Holocaust. Think about the universality. I had all these languages in my workroom.

The people in the building where I rented a little basement for La Mama were furious that a colored was living amongst them. Somebody called the Health Department and told them that prostitution was going on in the building and that a Negress had entertained sixteen white men in five hours. Well, many young men were helping me, building, putting the floor in, trying to make this little place into a room.

An elderly man came with a summons for my arrest. We told him what we were about and he turned out to be a person from vaudeville. So he says, ''Listen, become a restaurant and you can get a license.'' He asked what our name was for the place. My nickname has always been ''Mama,'' so he wrote that down and, laughing, said, ''Well, if you're gonna call it Mama, call it La Mama.'' And that's how we got the name.

We couldn't get critics to come and see our work down in that little basement. I thought playwrights deserved to be published, and when I would send the plays, I didn't have critiques and publishers would send them back and say we don't publish without critiques. I decided I would take my plays to Europe, get critiques there, and then come back and get them published.

So that's why in September, 1965, on a student ship, $118 one way, sixteen people sailed off with twenty-two plays. We slept in barns and fields, wherever we could. We played for room and board. The critics wrote that they didn't know what we were writing about or what we were talking about, that we could not act, but they liked us. By my going, I'm told, we started the whole circuit of the avant-garde.

I've never pretended to know anything about theater. I don't know how to read a script. I don't know the New York theater scene. Considering that we do at least forty productions every year and we've done that for years, just keeping up doesn't leave me very much time to go and see what somebody else is doing.

I'm not interested in the play. I'm interested in the person. If the person beeps, we do it. And if the play's a flop, I'm not bothered because I believe in that person.

In the beginning we used to pass the hat and whatever was in the hat was divided up by the actors. Sometimes the hat had something and then sometimes it didn't have anything.

The rent, costumes, and expenses I paid from my designing jobs. I used to work five and six jobs, running from one to the other because the more La Mama grew, the more money was needed. I worked myself into a state of exhaustion and the doctor said I had to give up one or the other. So I gave up the money and kept the theater.

The criticism that I get from foundations is that La Mama is an international theater and that we are not Americana. The criticism that I get from blacks is that La Mama is not a black theater. It was very difficult for me because, particularly in the sixties, La Mama was boycotted by blacks because I was not a black theater. My life was threatened. I think our public is about five percent black after twenty-five years.

One writer, who was a La Mama playwright, got to be ''minister of culture'' for the black movement. I would see him and he wouldn't speak to me, but he'd always call me up late that night and say, ''Mama, forgive me, I couldn't speak to you in front of my friend, but you're my mama.'' And he wasn't the only one. It was heavy, heavy.

I get invited to fly on my broom to all kinds of places to be with people to create, to make workshops. I went to Lebanon. La Mama's got a very strong following with the Druse, with the Shiites, with them all. La Mama's beloved in Syria. I worked with the Palestinians, the Israelis, got a huge contingent in Turkey. We have a big gold crown, an award from Korea. There's La Mama in Tokyo, in Melbourne. I slept out in the jungle with the pygmies. I've brought dancers from Zaire and Nigeria. There's an underground La Mama in Czechoslovakia. I've done extensive work in Rumania. There's been a La Mama group in Yugoslavia since 1966. I've had the good fortune to go to these places and be welcome.

Two years ago I got the MacArthur award. With that money I bought this property in Italy about two hours from Rome and I'm making a residence that will hold twenty-five artists. They can come and they won't have to pay for room and board. That's my dream.

Beah Richards

Born July 12, 1926, in Vicksburg, Mississippi

In my family the word *black* was always a beautiful word. It was a word that my father and mother used. When everybody was saying "Negro" and "colored," my family would use the term *black*. Many of the children used to fight over the word. What was it about the word *black* that made it such a trap for many people and such a wonderful trip for us?

Everybody in Vicksburg told me that I was going to be an actor. We didn't even have a theater, and if they had one, I couldn't go to it.

I came to New York in 1950 and I was there five years before I did my first Broadway show, which was *Take a Giant Step*, off-Broadway. I played the eighty-four-year-old grandmother with no makeup. When the show was over, I could walk right past people and they never knew. . . .

When people look only at the surface and that satisfies them and they think from that surface they see, that is to be truly blind. There is no blindness like that.

In 1962, when I came to do *The Amen Corner* by James Baldwin, the director, Frank Silvera, told me, "Don't act, just be." That's when I became an actor. I ran into this philosophy of being. I was a liberated person after that. I think before I was a reactor. Now I am an actor, I can take the initiative.

If you go inside where all people are and where the essence of their being is, you are not going to find anything to hang your prejudices on.

Race, what is that? Race is a competition, somebody winning and somebody losing. That's what we have translated it to be. But it is more like a family. If you can use my heart, my liver, or my eye, then we are more a family than a competition. Blood doesn't run in races! Come on!

The first play I wrote was called *All's Well that Ends*. It was about segregation. I did that because people put words in your mouth that have nothing to do with your life, your hopes, and aspirations. They were writing about "the Negro" and I was not "the Negro." I was a black person.

I came along at a period when black writers were just being heard from. Most of the plays prior to the fifties were written *about* black people. In the fifties there were works *by* black people. You know, looking at something and letting it come out of you are two different things.

There are a lot of movies out there that I would hate to be paid to do, some real demeaning, real woman-denigrating stuff. It is up to women to change their roles. They are going to have to write the stuff and do it. And they will.

The time has come for a perception of compassion in this world. What is this orgy of hate we are going into and where is it going to lead us? If hate had been the motivating thing in my life, I would be dead.

I decided I wouldn't bring a child into this world for anything. I adore them but it's the repetitive suffering quality of life that I wouldn't want to see anybody go through. I can't stand to see children suffer.

We had great hope that education was really going to do it. But education was an indoctrination. Both class and race survived education, and neither should. What is education then? If it doesn't help a human being to recognize that humanity is humanity, what is it for? So you can make a bigger salary than other people?

If there is any equality now, it has been our struggle that put it there. Because they said, "All people are created equal." They said "all" and meant "some." They meant "white." All means all, sweetheart.

Beah Richards is an actress, poet, and playwright of special sensitivity. She was nominated for an Oscar for her portrayal of the passionately peacemaking mother in the film Guess Who's Coming to Dinner? *Among her numerous credits for stage, television, and film are featured roles in James Baldwin's* The Amen Corner, *Ossie Davis's* Purlie Victorious, *and Lillian Hellman's* The Little Foxes. *In 1988, she won an Emmy award for her performance in* Frank's Place. *She lives in California, but returned to her hometown of Vicksburg, Mississippi, in 1998 to be honored for her distinguished career in theater and film by the Delta Sigma Theta Sorority. She also came out of retirement in 1998 to play a featured role in the film production of Toni Morrison's Pulitzer Prize-winning novel,* Beloved.

Carrie Saxon Perry

Born August 30, 1931, in Hartford, Connecticut

My high school, Hartford High, is the second oldest high school in the country. We had the 350th anniversary recently. When I went there it was mostly white. I hate to go to reunions. Everybody remembers me because there were only a few of us, and I don't remember them.

We are a classic urban center in that we have the tale of two cities. We have this magnificent downtown that is flourishing as a real financial center. And then we have high unemployment. We have the distinction of being the fourth poorest city and the fourth highest in the country in crime.

When I went to school, I really didn't know I was disadvantaged till I read about it. I knew who I was, I knew I was black, and I knew it was important that I excel with an education, because that was a way out. When people want their children to succeed, they don't tell you to go out and rob a bank. They say go and get an education, right?

My preparation for school was a major operation. I had to look right so there would never be anything about my appearance and I could just deal with education. After bathing, blacks have a tendency to be ashy, so you put on a little oil. I was so well oiled I could have almost slid to school.

When we moved to a project, we thought it was like moving on up, because we lived in a cold-water flat before and they had central heating in the project.

The projects were keeping people oppressed but they were disguised as a step up. Strange thing about oppression, you always believe that the oppressor is going to be a good guy. And it ain't so.

So many things in the system create an underclass, and the projects are one of them. That's the definition of poverty. The less choice you have, the poorer you are.

My definition of integration is that it broadens choice. It doesn't mean you just jump over the fence and try to do everything with other folks.

I had very strong women role models in my mother, my grandmother, and my aunt. They used to say, "When you fall down, get up. If you fall down again, get up. And don't be ashamed of falling down."

I started working in community action, organizing and trying to empower community groups. The neighborhood was becoming increasingly black and a white person—he was a good guy—was running for the State House. It was 1976. I didn't know nothing about politics and what you do. Me and my son, we just jumped in and did it. I was not endorsed by a single soul. I won on the machine. We were partying, just dancing and everything, and then they came in with the absentee ballots and said, "You lost." It was kind of crushing.

In the campaign debate one of the things we talked about was his experience versus my inexperience. I said, "I have a right to go up there and make a fool of myself. I'll never know until I get up there. If you're going to always judge people—women, blacks, Indians, whatever—against a white person who has had more advantages, more opportunities, and a quicker starting time, then we should never participate in anything."

The next time [1980] I ran against a black lawyer. Nobody endorsed me again and I won that time. I stayed in the State Legislature for seven years after that.

I don't know if I could have managed if I had not had those seven years as a state legislator. There were 186 folks with whom you had to deal in order to get an agenda. So it's all in persuasion, in information and doing your homework, it's all in understanding another person's point of view.

This is a difficult position because I have to make things happen through the force of my personality. Most power is illusionary and perceptual. You have to create an environment in which people perceive you as having some power.

I think there is a strong feeling that I'm a people's mayor. I wanted human services out of the closet. It had long been neglected. We're talking about teenage pregnancy, day care, substance-abuse rehab, remedial education, all those kinds of things. And our budget reflects that.

It's always difficult when you get a leadership position and it's not traditionally been held by a woman or a black or a dwarf, whatever. People have a real hard time adapting to change. But if you're sitting at the table, a representative government table, that person is going to have to adapt a little bit. So just my being here, my fight to be here, did it. And it's a continuum. For the next person it will be easier.

Racism is humorous now. They make these lousy jokes, and it's a racist joke, and they want you to laugh. They're called watermelon jokes, like to show that they're all for real—it's a real fun time. And it's deadly. The racism will continue. The coping will improve.

I believe that you have to force change. It doesn't always have to be by violence. You rebel, you organize, you force issues, you threaten the status quo, you show numbers, you promise upheaval: there are numbers of things you have to do. You have to be committed to long distance and accept the fact that it doesn't happen overnight, and that you're doing it probably for another generation.

Elected mayor of Hartford, the capital of Connecticut, in 1987, Carrie Perry was the first black woman mayor of a major U.S. city. She held office until 1992, when she was defeated in the general election. A social worker and a group home leader for ten years, she had been elected to the Connecticut State Assembly in 1980, and was reelected to that office three times. Shortly after leaving her mayoral office, she dedicated herself to work as an advocate for people on welfare. As an independent contractor, she has been developing programs, contacting state and local action groups, and presenting proposals on behalf of people in need of public assistance.

Charlayne Hunter-Gault

Born February 27, 1942, in Due West, South Carolina

Charlayne Hunter was one of two black students to desegregate the University of Georgia in Athens in 1961. She worked as a journalist for The New Yorker *and* The New York Times *before joining* The MacNeil/Lehrer NewsHour *as national correspondent in 1978. She has received two Emmy awards, and in 1986 was the recipient of the George Foster Peabody Award for Excellence in Broadcast Journalism for "Apartheid's People," a report on South Africa. Her autobiography,* In My Place, *was published in 1992. In 1997, after nineteen years as a* NewsHour *correspondent, Hunter (now Hunter-Gault) moved to Johannesburg, South Africa, and is now National Public Radio's chief correspondent for Africa.*

If you've ever been in the middle of a riot or the eye of a hurricane, you know it's very calm. It is. That is exactly how I felt the night of the riot. . . .

White students had been out there the night before yelling, and it was part of the resistance ritual, "Two, four, six, eight, we don't want to integrate." It sounded almost playful and then it got louder and louder and louder. And that's when the brick came through the window. I realized what had happened and it was like, "Wow! There is a riot in my room."

I probably didn't get frightened about it until ten or fifteen years later.

I think maybe that is part of what helps me in my journalism. I have a tremendous capacity to be detached but at the same time to be engaged.

Even in the best high school in Atlanta, we had hand-me-down textbooks and our labs were certainly not as well equipped. So the fact that we were prepared to compete in the way that we did was a minor miracle that the black schools accomplished.

That was the critical difference. We didn't want to go to school with white people—that wasn't it. It was those facilities they had.

There were real conflicts between Hamilton [Holmes, the other "first" black student] and me over our approach to the whole situation. I was really much more interested in integrating the place and Hamp was much more interested in desegregation.

It got to be bigger than I ever thought it would be. I didn't expect that. People wanted us to be perfect, I guess. And I wanted to be me, which was an imperfect person.

There was conflict and there was pain. There was crisis and there was ignorance and all of that. But I emerged as a whole person and the university came out the better for it.

The university itself has a lot of unfinished business. The young people have a lot of complaints and knowing how far they've come should not mitigate their demands for a more equitable piece of the state pie.

I was able to advance at *The New Yorker* because I could write. And so, like everybody else, when I wasn't licking envelopes and stuffing rejection letters and typing schedules, I was working on some little piece at lunchtime at my desk. I had some wonderful opportunities and I am not ungrateful, but I would still be there licking envelopes if I hadn't had some kind of talent that I was willing to work hard at and get people to help me develop.

You have to assess every situation that you're in and you have to decide, is this happening because I'm black? Is this happening because I'm a woman? Or is this happening because this is how it happens?

Whatever I have faced as a woman is probably a lot more subtle than what I have faced as a black person. We did find out, for example, at *The New York Times*, that women across the board were making less money than most men. And there was a successful lawsuit. But the same thing happened with blacks. And there was also a successful lawsuit.

I have never looked on being black or being a woman as a handicap and, honestly, I have used those things to my advantage, in the workplace particularly.

I have never apologized for doing black stories, being interested in black stories, and insisting that every institution that I work for report black stories.

I think the South has a much greater opportunity than the North to right some of the historic wrongs.

People have been lying in the North about race relations as long as I've been here. I haven't seen that many integrated schools, and yet I have seen a lot that are as segregated as the one I went to.

Integration has some negative by-products as well. It has helped to dilute some of the institutions where we have had this tremendous reservoir of confidence-building and strength—the black colleges, the churches, the family.

So there is good news and bad news. The good news is that you do begin to see some commitment to change. The bad news is that you've got to chip away at the concrete of institutional racism.

South Africa is one of the greatest challenges that we in the media face. We are being manipulated by the South African government. Just beginning to contemplate what could happen in South Africa if the world can't watch is an awesome proposition. This is not a totally appropriate analogy, but if television had been there, could the Holocaust have happened?

Whatever you say about this country, we do have a Constitution where equality of opportunity is a basic principle. We have problems living up to it, but it is there in the Constitution, which isn't the case in South Africa.

If people are informed they will do the right thing. It's when they are not informed that they become hostages to prejudice.

Constance Baker Motley

Born September 14, 1921, in New Haven, Connecticut

I grew up in New Haven in a community where people worked. Our house was like a halfway house for people coming from Nevis, an island in the Caribbean where my parents—and Alexander Hamilton—were born. Everybody we knew worked at Yale washing dishes or waiting on tables or whatever. Nevisians believed in helping each other. There was no sitting around doing nothing.

We always lived in an integrated neighborhood and I always went to integrated schools. There were very few blacks in New Haven at that time so we didn't encounter a great deal of hostility from the whites. In fact, many were patronizing. They did things for blacks. That was the thing to do.

It was 1940, and I had finished high school and wasn't in college. A very successful businessman who had built a community center for blacks was very concerned about getting black people to use it more. When he had a meeting to hear from people in the community, I said I thought the reason blacks were not participating was because they were not on the board of directors. To many black adults that was an insensitive thing to say. They viewed me as a young person who just didn't know how to act.

The next day I got a call from the black director of the community center to go see this businessman, Clarence Blakeslee. He said he would be glad to pay for my college education. He asked me what I wanted to be. I said I wanted to be a lawyer. He didn't believe that women could make it in law, but he figured that if I had that ambition who was he to say no. So he said, "Just let me know when you're ready to go."

I finished college [Fisk and New York University] in two and a half years and Columbia Law School in 1946. Yes, he was able to see me finish.

You can't invent events. They just happen. But you have to be prepared to deal with them when they happen.

When I was in my senior year at Columbia I got a job as a clerk with Thurgood Marshall, who was then the head of the NAACP Legal Defense Fund. For me that was a stroke of luck because I got in on the ground floor of the civil rights legal revolution.

I got a chance to actually try cases, argue cases in the Courts of Appeal and the United States Supreme Court. You know, the average lawyer never even sees the Supreme Court, let alone gets to argue a case there.

I was a part of a civil rights movement, involved in spectacular legal victories which we are not going to duplicate in this century. In the next century, there may be some other movement equally spectacular in terms of legal decisions, but the Supreme Court decisions of 1954 to '64 are exceptional in terms of their constitutional significance. In one case after the other, segregation was stricken as unconstitutional. This resulted in a revolution in this country—a social revolution.

Birmingham in 1954 and '55, that was a scary place. Now it has emerged and they have a black mayor. I never thought I would live long enough to see that much change.

I think the Meredith case was the most frightening, because we had no protection. James Meredith [in 1962 the first black to attend the University of Mississippi] believed that he was going to be shot and killed in the black community by some black paid to kill him.

When you see black people on television brushing their teeth with Colgate like everybody else, that says much more than any civil rights activist or orator. When whites turn on television and see black people the same as white people, subconsciously they are accepting this tremendous change which has come into society.

The suggestion that women should be equal and have a job that a man might have touches people in a very sensitive way. It is not as readily accepted as the idea of equality for blacks; I think there is much more trouble with that. That's a really deep revolution.

Had I been economically successful, that would have been a problem for my husband. But I wasn't any threat because I wasn't making any money. When I was working for the NAACP, in the very early days, I'd have to borrow lunch money from him.

I don't know any of my classmates at Columbia who have been particularly successful. Financially, I guess some have. But they don't see their names in law books. I do. I feel good about that.

The demand of people going into the legal profession today is to be well prepared educationally. Two law clerks that I had had PhDs, then they went to law school. That's the kind of competition you're talking about.

The idea of getting greater political power is something which young blacks are concentrating on. Someday there'll be a black governor in Georgia and all the other southern states where they have large black populations. Something which we think is impossible now is not impossible in another decade.

When President Lyndon Johnson appointed Constance Baker Motley to the United States District Court in 1966, she became the first black woman to serve as a federal judge. One of the courtroom tacticians of the Civil Rights Movement, she worked for twenty years with the NAACP Legal Defense Fund. She was the only woman elected to the New York State Senate in 1964, and was Manhattan borough president for the years 1965–1966. Beginning in 1982, she served four years as Chief Judge of the Southern District of New York, and assumed senior judge status in 1986. Judge Motley is one of the most honored women in the legal profession. She has received twenty-nine honorary doctorate degrees and was inducted into the National Women's Hall of Fame, Seneca, New York, in 1993. She is the author of Equal Justice Under Law: An Autobiography, *published in 1998.*

69

Oprah Winfrey

Born January 29, 1954, in Kosciusko, Mississippi

Oprah Winfrey makes a difference in people's lives. "Oprah's Book Club" has made instant best sellers of the Club's selections, while her "Angel Network" has offered disadvantaged students college tuition through donations of her audience's "spare change." The National Academy of Television Arts & Sciences has presented her show with a total of 32 Emmy awards and, in 1998, honored Winfrey with its "Lifetime Achievement Award." She received the coveted George Foster Peabody "Individual Achievement Award" in 1996. Her personal fortune is estimated to be over a half billion dollars. Her company, Harpo Entertainment Group, creates and produces television shows, home videos, and feature films, including the 1998 screen adaptation of Toni Morrison's Beloved, *in which Winfrey stars as "Sethe." In 1991, her testimony before the U.S. Judiciary Committee initiated the national Child Protection Act, and what became known nationally as "the Oprah Bill" became law in 1993.*

One of the greatest assets I have is good timing. I had the good timing to be born in 1954, the year of *Brown v. Board of Education*. I'm a product of desegregation. That has enabled me to become as successful as I have, financially, emotionally, and spiritually.

I am grateful and blessed because those women whose names made the history books, and a lot who did not, are all bridges that I've crossed over to get to this side. I stand here on solid ground because of them. I am a product of every other black woman before me who has done or said anything worthwhile. Recognizing that I am a part of that history is what allows me to soar.

I was raised to believe that excellence is the best deterrent to racism or sexism. And that's how I operate my life.

It never occurred to me that I was less than anybody else, because I was always ahead of everybody else. I never thought that I was a pretty girl because I thought you had to be light-skinned, have a pointed nose and thin lips in order to be pretty. The thought of being pretty was a foreign idea to me. So I decided to be smart instead.

When I was seven or eight years old, I moved to Nashville to live with my father and my stepmother, who had me reading five books every two weeks. Had vocabulary lists for me to learn. That's how I was brought up on black literature and black people who had succeeded.

In 1968 I was confused by it all. I was angry because in Milwaukee where I lived then they were burning things down in our neighborhoods. I remember pulling up a shade and there was a National Guardsman on our front porch. He turned around with a gun. I was terrified. It was like our neighborhood was under siege.

I went to college [Tennessee State] and was ostracized because I was not militant and I was not angry. Part of the reason was because I wasn't aware enough to be angry. As an adult, I'm far angrier than I was coming up.

I think that education is power. I think that being able to communicate with people is power. One of my main goals on the planet is to encourage people to empower themselves. I do that through my work on television and my work socially with organizations and my work in my relationships. I do think that the greatest lesson of life is that you are responsible for your own life.

I'm surprisingly healthy, mentally healthy. I never internalized sexual abuse as being this awful thing that had happened to me. I know most women carry it, the anger, the guilt, and they use it for the rest of their lives. But no need to. I'm neither guilty nor angry.

I don't buy into the whole criticism of the show being sensational, because life is sensational. Life is incredible, bizarre, weird, and sensational.

I am interested in discovering new things, period. I don't have to pretend to be interested. I don't like fake anything or faking anything. That's probably why the show does as well as it does. It's as easy as breathing.

I've interviewed the Klan and skinheads and those people. They really don't make me angry. I genuinely feel sorry. When people stand up and call me "nigger," it does not make me angry. I know that for a person to stand up and say that to me means they have a miserable life. I know that you cannot hate other people without hating yourself.

For a lot of people, I recognize that I carry their dreams. When they see me, they see themselves. And it's all right for me to make a million dollars because they can conceive of themselves making a million. They can't conceive making 20 million or 50 million. It's too much.

I don't fit other people's expectations. It is a source of inspiration to a lot of black people. I think it also instills fear in other black people. Once somebody who looks like me makes it, then what? It all boils down to self-hatred. That's the source of all problems on the planet, actually. It certainly is the source of every problem on my show.

It seems like an untruth coming from somebody who obviously has a lot of material things, but I'm not controlled by the material things. I'm not defined by them at all. The only difference between being famous and not is that people know your name. That's all.

This show does great things for people. But my sense is that there are even greater things that I have been called to do.

It's very easy to get lazy when you get rich and forget where you came from. So the challenge is to never forget. You're here to do something, not just lay back and sit poolside. The challenge is to use this power, use this fame to help other people and do it in ways that are inspiring.

And that's why I've formed my own company. Rather than complain about television and get upset about it and angry, I decided I'd start changing it myself. The way to change it is to prove that people will respond to good work. If you give people something good to watch, if you uplift them, enlighten them, encourage them, as well as entertain them, they will respond to it. That's just part of the spirit.

Sonia Sanchez

Born September 9, 1934, in Birmingham, Alabama

Sonia Sanchez has written poetry, short stories, plays, and children's books. Prolific and controversial, she has been a skillful innovator in the use of urban Black English, eloquent profanity, and colorfully precise imagery. Titles of some of her sixteen works are We a BaddDDD People *(1970),* A Blues Book for Blue Black Magical Women *(1974), and* I've been a Woman: New and Selected Poems *(1981). A recipient of the Governor's Award for Humanities in Pennsylvania in 1988, she is the Laurel Carnel Professor of English and Chairperson of the Women's Studies Program at Temple University. A world traveler, she's read her poetry, and lectured before audiences as widespread as China and Africa, and at more than 500 universities and colleges in the United States. Her 1998 book,* Does Your House Have Lions? *was a finalist for the National Book Critics Circle Award.*

I was about eight when we moved from Birmingham to Harlem. In the junior high school when they stood up in assembly to sing the national anthem my sister and I sang "Lift Every Voice and Sing." That's what we sang in Birmingham, Alabama.

I used to say in glib fashion in my 1960s days, "I write because that way I don't kill anyone." It was oh, so dramatic. But I write to keep in contact with our ancestors and to spread truth to people.

I was blessed in my time to be involved with all the literary people and all the political people, honestly involved, working, rolling-up-sleeves working, driving out of southern towns fastly fast or driving out of western towns fastly fast down the peninsula in California with no headlights on because after what you had said from poetry readings, people were mad at you and were following you out of town.

We were playing the dozens with America, we were talking about America. But the ones doing the reviewing had not studied our folklore or our people well enough to understand. Any person reading me, steeped in black literature, knew what we were saying. It was funny in a very real sense.

Quite often you find poets saying things that people are afraid to say, and you take the weight. But I had good shoulders to climb on.

I was at Hunter College from 1951 to 1955. We were that generation that was very quiet. The first thing I got involved in was New York CORE. We thought we were the most militant things around. At the time, everyone thought Malcolm was a racist. I am not a revisionist. We tend to reinvent memory sometimes, for our own convenience. He frightened most people. When he came on the scene, everybody would kind of pull the shade and say, "I won't let this light inside at all. Period."

We must never underestimate what Muslims did for blacks in making them look at themselves. The Nation of Islam was very important to the movement of black folks going from Negro to black, bringing the whole sense of doing for yourself and loving yourself.

Negro is an interesting word. This country couldn't call us Africans because if it had, we would have understood some things about ourselves. We would not have been "this Negro in America," constantly enslaved even after slavery. It would have given us a sense of continuity. So they had to say colored and Negro and nigger to keep us in our place, to remind us that we were only from this country.

When I get up and preach or give a talk in a church, I always say that my grandmother, who was the deaconess in our church, never could do this, but now I can. So I am carrying on the spirit and energy of all those old sisters from the church who used to gather in my grandmother's home where they would be seated all day snapping beans, making their cakes for sale, making the potatoes or whatever to take home with them.

I found out about people from listening to them. I would sneak behind the couch and sit there. My grandmother knew I was there, and she let me listen. There was something that she was passing on to me that I didn't, at the time, understand. I found out that our tribe did not allow anyone to abuse them.

I think the first time most black children found out they were black was through a negative experience. Years later when I had children, I said I would never let them discover that they are black via a negative incident. You kind of rock them in blackness, and hum to them and say, "Isn't this great that you are this pretty little black child I'm holding here?"

I had no memory of my mother. She died when I was one year old, giving birth to twins. So, of course, I give birth to twins thirty years later. I'm doing a novel and in it I go back into my mother's womb. That's how I get to know her and have a conversation with her and her mother. It's a novel about how women must know themselves before they go out and get into a relationship. They must know from whence they've come—that history of women—otherwise, the relationship will be a disaster.

When I teach literature, I teach the sociology of it and the economics of it also. Quite often, in a classroom, many women see how similar their oppressions have been. You will see how incest has permeated the lives of women—black women, white women, whatever—and the silence about that.

What we learn in our classroom is unbelievable. That's why I love teaching, the kind of joy of teaching where you make people jump barriers and touch each other.

If you hook into honors, you could hook into being disappointed. So I hook into people and into my work. And if I am honored, I give it back to people, "I do this for you because I know your voices."

I've always heard music of some kind when I write.

I love rocking chairs. I have them all over the house. I just sit and rock for hours, just to think. As one old woman said, "I loves to think."

Georgia Montgomery Davis Powers

Born October 19, 1923, in Springfield, Kentucky

I was an only girl with eight boys. We had what we needed, but we didn't have everything we wanted. My parents thought the boys could do everything and they thought I should stay in the house. My father taught all the boys how to work on cars, all how to drive, but not me. Now, I knew I was different from the boys, but I still wanted to know what was going on.

I did work as a riveter on airplane fuselages in Buffalo, New York. After about three months, they came to me and asked me if I would like to be an expediter. I didn't know what it was. I didn't even know what the word was. I said, "Is it a promotion?" They said, "Yes." "Well, I'll take it." So that's just been the story of my life.

After I had moved to Louisville a member of my church asked me if I'd be interested in getting involved in a political campaign. I said, "Oh, no, I don't know anything about politics. I just vote." I told the campaign manager that I'd never worked in politics before but I'd work one week. I said, "If I don't like it, I won't be back." After I had been there two days, they put me in the position of chairing the volunteers. It worked very well. From 1962 to 1967, I worked right there for one candidate after the other in campaign headquarters.

I didn't know what I wanted to do until I was forty-five, and it was politics. I counted up the number of jobs I had had until that time. It was at least thirty. You do a lot of things, sometimes, before you can decide what you want to do. I found that I had been the first black telephone operator in Buffalo.

I ran for office in 1967. Having worked in other campaigns, I had learned how to organize precincts, how to get endorsements, and how to win elections. I kept my mouth shut and my eyes and ears open.

The first bill I introduced was an open housing bill. I had a seatmate who had been there a few years before I got there. He was nice to me in that he taught me the procedure in the Senate. When I would get up to speak on a bill, if I talked too long, he'd just kind of pull my dress-tail and say, "Sit down. You know, you're killing your bill."

Dr. Martin Luther King, Jr. called and asked me if I would come to Memphis to help them with the sanitation workers' strike. We got to Memphis late on April 3 [1968] and we sat there at the Lorraine Motel and talked till about four o'clock in the morning. It was Dr. King, Dr. Ralph Abernathy, and some others. Just laughing and talking. A. D. [Rev. A. D. King, Dr. King's brother] was in the conversation. Black preachers have a commonality that others don't have. They joke with each other. They called me G. D. instead of Georgia 'cause all the preachers had initials—A. D., M. L.

April 4 was just a relaxed day. We were all ready to go out to dinner. "A soul thing," Dr. King said.

I was standing there at the mirror just sort of pushing my hair into place. I heard a lot of voices out in the courtyard—Jesse Jackson, staff people, Hosea Williams. I was thinking, "I'll just wait outside until Dr. King comes down," when I heard the shot. And it was so loud. Immediately I heard a woman scream, "Oh, my god! They shot Dr. King."

I went right out the door. Where were all the people who had been in the courtyard, I wondered. Well, they had taken cover. And then I looked up and saw him. . . .

It's the only time I've ever been in shock like that. I couldn't get warm. We were going to move from the Lorraine but we had to spend the night back there. Everybody was in a state of shock. I think sometimes I'm still in shock.

I think the greatest effect he had on me was to see how humble he was. I saw him talk to the lowliest of persons. He would stop in the middle of a demonstration, leave the march, and go to the side to talk to someone. I learned to take time out to talk, regardless.

I heard someone tell someone that I'm manipulative. Well, that's sorta kinda natural with a politician.

When I'd get to the Senate floor, I'd pray first. Prayer has really been the key for me. I was not qualified for this position. I had no training whatsoever. Having been successful for twenty-one years, it had to be something, something more powerful than what I am.

All the legislation dealing with civil rights, sex discrimination, job discrimination, age discrimination, all that I have promoted since I've been in the legislature—I found in twenty years I'm the only one who has introduced anything related to civil rights.

I was thinking, when am I going to realize that sixty-five is supposed to be old? I don't know when I'm going to act my age.

In 1967, Georgia Davis Powers became the first woman and the first black person to be elected to the Kentucky State Senate. During her five four-year terms, she pressed for legislation on public accommodations, fair employment, open housing, and other issues of special concern to women, children, and the poor. She was an active participant in several historic demonstrations and was one of the organizers of the Kentucky affiliate of the Southern Christian Leadership Conference. In 1988, she declined to run for reelection and stepped away from an illustrious political career. She shares the details of that career, including her personal and political encounters with men, in her controversial book, I Shared the Dream: The Pride, Passion and Politics of the First Black Woman Senator from Kentucky, *published in 1995.*

Daisy Bates

Born November 11, 1914, in Huttig, Arkansas

My mother was a beautiful woman, dark, mixed Indian and Negro. I found out early in my childhood what happened to her. When I was a baby she was raped and murdered by three white men one night. Before my father went to look for her, he took me to his best friend's house and said, "Keep her until I come back." My father never came back. His friend adopted me. Later I was told, "You might as well learn now that if a white man wants you, he'll take you."

Once I was sent to the store to get some pork chops. I was happy, dressed up, you know, proud that I was trusted. I told the butcher, "I'd like a pound of center-cut pork chops, if you please." He just took my dollar. I was the only person in

there at that time, but a little white girl came in and he served her, gave her a nice center-cut pork chop. Then a woman walked up and he served her. I asked again and he said, "Niggers have to wait until all the whites have been served." Then he gave me a handful of bad meat and told me to go on, that I had no money.

I was so mad and hurt. When my daddy came home, I told him the story. I wanted to go back there and make that butcher give me the kind of meat I wanted. He said, "It's not so bad." I asked him, "Daddy, are you afraid?" I never saw him so angry. He said, "Haven't you heard what I've been trying to tell you? I could be killed and nothing would be done about it." Killed over a pork chop. And more than

head with my .38 and he ducked and dropped it. Another night the police caught some people with guns and ammunition enough to blow the whole town away. Dynamite, everything. I was asked to stay with friends someplace else. I said, "Why should I? This is my home. I live here, I'm gonna stay here."

I didn't want anybody killed in the process. The whole movement would have been lost and all that suffering that the children had gone through would have been lost.

The kids were so courageous. They were ready to go and they wanted to go. The whites didn't want them and it made them want to go more. One of the reasons President Eisenhower was so long making up his mind was because he didn't want to be embarrassed sending in federal troops if the kids would not go in.

I think the high point was when the troops came in and Minnie Jean Brown [one of the Little Rock Nine] smiled and said, "For the first time in my life I feel like an American citizen."

I was fighting from my understanding of the past. There were blacks that didn't understand what was happening to them. This disturbed me an awful lot. There were not enough people who wanted to change, not enough of them to fight for change.

I was independent. I didn't have a boss I had to please. I thought I was strong putting out thirty thousand papers all over the state.

We brought to the public the conditions of the system in the South. Heretofore when something happened to a Negro and it was difficult to get the facts, reporters went to the white people and took their word for everything. But this time they had to come to me, here. They got the message.

We were in court in 1956 and I wanted to go to the rest room outside the judge's chambers. I was in a hurry and I didn't see the Whites Only sign. A charwoman, a white woman, was down on her knees cleaning up vomit. She said, "Nigger, you're in the wrong place." I went on in and used the rest room. When I came around she was still there on her knees. I was so angry with her I could have pushed her head down in the bucket. But I realized she was as much a victim as I was. I felt sorry for her.

I don't think I was courageous. I think I was determined.

I've gotten awards and plaques. I think they are saying, "You are doing what I'd like to do but I can't do it because I gotta eat, I gotta feed my kids."

Changes have been made. The people who were quiet are now speaking out. But I realize that you cannot erase in thirty years what it took two hundred years to establish.

that, he said that Mother and I would be the next victims.

I can remember what my daddy said on his dying day. "Daisy," he said, "you're consumed with hatred for white people." He said, "If you're gonna hate, make it count for something. Hate segregation in the South."

When we took on segregation in the Little Rock schools I don't think we had any big idea that we were gonna win it then. But they were gonna know they had had a fight!

The phone rang constantly with threats. They broke the windows with rocks. They burned crosses in the yard all the time. Huge ones. And they set the house on fire. One night a man was going to throw a Molotov cocktail. I shot over his

Daisy Bates, along with her husband L. C. Bates, established a weekly newspaper, The Arkansas State Press, in the early 1940s. Elected president of the Arkansas NAACP, she led the historic fight of the Little Rock Nine to desegregate Central High School in 1957. Her book, The Long Shadow of Little Rock, was published in 1962. Mrs. Bates remains a major figure in the fight for school integration. Her actions shaped the social and educational history of this nation at a moment of constitutional crisis. Through the efforts of a local ministerial alliance, her home in Little Rock has become a national museum.

Marva Nettles Collins

Born August 31, 1936, in Monroeville, Alabama

I grew up in a very nurtured background. I never had to worry about money, clothing, and things. My dad and I were very close friends. I could ask him questions and we would sit and talk until the wee hours of the morning.

When my dad would see black women walking to work in the mornings, I used to hear him give off a litany of words, saying he would die before he let his family work in the kitchens of white folks.

If you went to college in Alabama, you were a celebrity. The minister had you stand in church and all the people would give you a quarter or fifty cents, what they could. You didn't get into trouble because in your mind's eye you could see all those people caring about you, depending on you.

This school is all about service. Every child has to tutor five other children in their neighborhood. It's part of our motto: Entrance to learn, exit to serve.

We have a saying here that each of us checks our ego at the door in the morning when we come in. There is no place here for majestic egos.

We teach our children here. When they give us sloppy work, we ask them, "Would you give this to God?" And if they say, "No," we say, "We don't want it either." If it's sloppy, it goes in the garbage pail. "I love you very much, but this is where it goes. Now, do it over."

I've always said that with my own children. I disagree with you right now but I love you all the time.

I get a real kick out of a real tough kid because I know that I'm going to break him. We had a white kid last year that was seventeen and his mother landed up here from South Carolina. Eric was very hostile. He had been put down, he couldn't read, and one day he called me a jungle bunny. I said, "Sweetheart, when you learn to read, write, and spell jungle bunny, Mrs. Collins will take offense to it. Right now I love you." And he had to learn how to read, write, and spell those words.

I've seen brilliant kids labeled "learning disabled" because a teacher didn't know what to do with them. The question that always lurks in my mind is, What would I do if this was my child?

We talk about violence in the classroom, but no one ever mentions a teacher grabbing a kid. That's part of this discipline problem. You just don't grab a kid unless you have established some rapport with him first. I can grab them, but I love them first.

Schools are bad all over this country. You can actually get through high school in America by knowing how to make T for true and F for false and check marks. . . .

I don't know whether we in this country have become anesthetized or we're suffering from senility.

We are going to have to try to have our own high school because our children have problems when they leave here. They learn to shut up, they learn to fake it. Here they are free, free to disagree with me.

In here the children correct us. They'll say, "Mrs. Collins, that's wrong, you made a mistake." And I'll say, "You are so bright, I want to be just like you when I grow up."

I can never teach your children everything they need to know. But I can teach them to be curious and discontent.

Every child in this school has the greatest respect in the world. I never have to raise my voice and scream because I am what I want them to be.

I don't want to be wealthy. I don't need that kind of power. Power is when I walk into this school and these little kids' eyes hold wonder like a cup.

I think what everybody calls a miracle is just common sense, really. You can look at the attitudes when people come in. That's why they call it a miracle. These are black kids and they're not supposed to know the things they know and achieve the way they are achieving.

I think it is very interesting that teachers from monied systems all over the world come into this very spartan facility to learn our methodology. I cannot change the world, but I do not have to conform.

What I do concerns me, not what people think. There is a line one of my children told a white kid once. We had taken them to a play and the white kid called one of them a nigger. The little nine-year-old looked and said, "No wise man will insult me and no fool can." I've always remembered that. I learn from children too. . . .

Our kids change their parents. These kids are going to be the new order emerging in our society.

Marva Collins founded Westside Preparatory School in Chicago in 1975 to educate the children of the city's mean streets. Using pension funds from fourteen years of teaching in public schools, she built a schoolroom in her home. That school, which now occupies two buildings, grew from eighteen students to 250, and from skepticism to success, partly with the help of proceeds from the 1981 television movie, The Marva Collins Story. *In 1996, Marva Collins went to the Chicago Public School system to ask for three of the 109 schools placed on probation by Chicago education authorities. The three were the lowest achieving, in the worst locations, and had the least parental involvement. The improvement process has ended with well-measured success. Collins is the recipient of more than forty-two honorary degrees from colleges and universities across the country. as well as the prestigious Jefferson Award for the Greater Public Service Benefiting the Disadvantaged.*

Lena Horne

Born June 30, 1917, in Brooklyn, New York

My grandmother [my father's mother] said, "Don't let anybody see you cry. Hold your head up very straight, look at people, and answer them or question them distinctly." And then her woman's thing would come out because she'd say, "Don't be as weak as your mother." Well, that was the fight that strengthened me, because I would take up for my mother.

I wanted to be a teacher. I got sidetracked through my mother into show business. My grandmother couldn't bear it that my mother was on the stage. In those days, we were freaks, and my mother was a freak. There was no respect for her. My mother had this crazy idea about me being a star. She didn't understand anything. *Her* mother had raised her to be a little princess.

My grandmother took me to her meetings from the time I was little until I was fifteen. She was in the Urban League, the NAACP, and the Ethical Culture Society. I was surrounded by adult activities. I'm glad because if I hadn't had that from her, then the other side of my life, which was more bleak, might have finished me.

My father was a gambler and a racketeer. Because he knew how loathsome life was, he taught me a lot. He gave me all the street knowledge I needed to survive.

My father used to have these old sayings like, "Don't trust no bush that quivers." He paid off the cops and was allowed to run his rackets. He used to say, "Don't whine, pay the bill," if you owe it.

Out there in Hollywood, I was completely isolated. I went through some funny times because they didn't know what black people were like. Me and the shoeshine boy were the only two black people out there at the studio, most every day.

My father had scared them to death. I think that was the first time a black man had ever come into Louis B. Mayer's office and said, "I don't want my daughter in this mess." There was all this kind of crap that, in our business, particularly, is sexual. He was so articulate and so beautiful, they just said, "Well, don't worry." And they didn't know what to do with me.

I was unique in that I was a kind of black that white people could accept. I was their daydream. I had the worst kind of acceptance because it was never for how great I was or what I contributed. It was because of the way I looked.

I made a couple of stands out there at MGM and I was encouraged on the surface. But the very people that I had admired and written to for advice to turn down these parts, were sending their sisters or their cousins.

It took me many years to be able to sing, because I wasn't a natural singer. I could carry a tune, but that was about it.

My own people didn't see me as a performer because they were busy trying to make a living and feed themselves. Until I got to Café Society in the forties, I didn't even have a black audience and then it was mixed.

I was always battling the system to try to get to be with my people. Finally, I wouldn't work for places that kept us out. I couldn't get a place to live, so I fought for housing. The mere fact of living had to be fought, because I was black and I never lost sight of that.

Until I struck this man in a nightclub in Hollywood [for his racist insult], I never knew that anybody knew anything about me. I got telegrams from black people saying, "How wonderful, we didn't know." I just automatically thought that black people knew that if you were black, you were going to catch hell. They thought because I was me that I wasn't catching hell.

It was a damn fight everywhere I was, every place I worked, in New York, in Hollywood, all over the world.

When I was sent South early, I lived with people who existed on leavings from white people's tables. Then, in the sixties, when I went South, when I went back and found people that had taken care of me when I was a little girl, I found that I was a part of something bigger than myself.

The impact of them killing Medgar Evers hit me so hard because I saw him and his wife doing, God, this fantastic work in that place. It brought me back to life. Then I belonged, finally. I think I earned my way back, but it was a rough process. Mississippi, it killed me, but it woke me up. And I cried for the first time in many years.

As an artist I had been very rigid and cold. When I sang in Mississippi, in a church there, my heart just broke. When I was with my own people, I began to be a better artist and performer. I turned my prejudice loose.

Don't be afraid to feel as angry or as loving as you can, because when you feel nothing, it's just death.

I'm glad I lived through the sixties, because that's the first time and the last time I saw a commingling of whites and blacks with an attitude that started out to be very right and very healthy. And then, of course, it was over. But I saw it and that did me a lot of good.

I never thought I'd live this long to see this kind of ruin, decimation. My own people are so disillusioned, desperate, and angry. Angrier than in the sixties, I think, except they have no place to put this anger.

Singer, actress, and legendary beauty, Lena Horne began her career at sixteen as a chorus girl at the Cotton Club in Harlem. Almost fifty years later she starred in a retrospective, Lena Horne: The Lady and Her Music, *the longest-running one-woman show in Broadway history. She performed in the 1940s film classics,* Cabin in the Sky *and* Stormy Weather, *and in the Broadway musical* Jamaica. *In 1984, she was honored by the Kennedy Center for lifetime achievement in the performing arts, and in 1987, she received the Pied Piper Award from the American Society of Composers, Authors and Publishers. Her 1995 album,* An Evening with Lena Horne, *recorded live, won a Grammy, and her most recent recording, the aptly titled* Being Myself, *was released the summer she turned 81—1998. Lena Horne was presented with the Essence Award in 1992, and Yale University awarded her an honorary Doctorate of Humane Letters on Memorial Day 1998.*

Willie Mae Ford Smith

Born June 23, 1904, in Rolling Fork, Mississippi
Died February 2, 1994, St. Louis, Missouri

Mother Smith, known as the mother of gospel music, traveled the country singing and preaching in a vibrant, intense style that was often in opposition to established church practices. She was one of the stars of the 1983 gospel film, Say Amen, Somebody. *In 1988, the National Endowment for the Arts awarded her a National Heritage Fellowship, recognizing her contribution as an outstanding American folk artist.*

My mother would sing "The Lonely Jesus" and it would sound so good to me. I'd sing "The Long-leg Jesus" 'cause I didn't know. I never got it different until I got to be a big girl. When I was little I'd get up on the table and sing, "There's not a friend like the long-leg Jesus, no no not one." People laughin' at me singin' that, but I thought they was feelin' good 'cause I was a child.

My mother was a wet-nurse, if you know what I mean. So many white people had babies that didn't have any milk, breast milk. My mother was just like a little dairy. She would get babies all the time. When I was a baby, my milk went to the other white kids and I got the strippings. . . .

They left Mississippi and came to Memphis and they left Memphis when [the United States entered] the war in 1917. At that time white folks were killin' black folks and black folks were killin' white folks. You get a black man mad, he thinks "You're just goin' to kill me. I'm goin' to die anyway. So I'm goin' to get you while I'm goin'. We goin' out together." My daddy didn't want to live in that circumstance so he thought he better push out with all his children, fourteen children—seven sisters and seven brothers. I happened to be the seventh of the fourteen children.

After I received the gift of the holy experience, I began to dig. It was a call of God. But I went to a seminary school for training. I knew how to read the Bible. You read the Bible with your eyes, of course, but you don't know how to get the connections.

When the bishop's son was fixing the program up for his father's funeral—who goin' to sing this and what—I told him I didn't want to sing that. He said, "But Dad liked that song." I said okay and I tried all I knew to get up there and sing it. I stood still and breathed a while and then he said, "Use what you got." I got this song in my heart and I sang it. That fitted me, it was a good garment for me. You sing what fits you.

The preachers would say about me, "Don't let her come in your church 'cause she's a bell cow. She'll lead all your people out acting that foolish stuff."

When I would go to their meetings, the preachers would say, "You can sit down there, you don't need to come up here. Don't get in my program. You a woman, didn't you realize?" No respect at all. Well, it don't make no difference to me. So I turn around in my pew and sing to that audience. Next thing I know, "Come on up here, get up and let all of them see you."

I felt like taking my number up the aisle, but you've got to use common sense with whatever you do. You see, when the spirit was taking me away, [one preacher] said, "Control yourself, because the Holy Spirit will use you up in one performance."

See, God don't want no filter on His work. To be a gospel singer, you got to be a gospel person. You know, some people will just woo everybody in church. They'll just dress so fabulous and frilly. People can't get the gospel for looking at you, you know. I don't worry about my fancy clothes. When I get up to carry on, I want to look so they won't wonder, what is that she got on?

I'm the mother of the world. All these children are mine. Anybody let me love 'em, they're mine. Those that don't let me love 'em, then I love 'em anyhow.

Yeah, they love me. I believe they do. If they don't love me, I don't want to find out.

God is not pleased. He's not pleased with all this shackin' business. He's not pleased with all this liquor business and dope. Slippin' and slidin', peepin' and hidin' don't work with God.

Look at the trees now, aren't they bare? But you let a certain day come for spring and they'll come out. They won't be the same leaves that was there last year, but when they come out they're so pretty. I look out at those trees and just think, Oh, you're so beautiful. God sure dressed you up. I say that to a tree. The work I have done, if I have to do it over, I'm willin'. But I don't want to go back. Let me be the leaf just laying at the foot of the tree giving it substance to grow.

When you're walkin' with God you don't worry about what you're gonna get in this life. I told you in my song—you heard it, didn't you? I'm gonna be happy. I'll tell you it makes me happy now when I think about the home over there. I don't need no washing, I don't need no maid. Oh, hallelujah! When I get over there, I believe I'm gonna get that milk and honey. I've read about it, heard about it. I've been taught about it. I want it! I want it! I want to go home with God and rest.

Some said I'm packin' up, gettin' ready to go. But I'm not! Honey, I'm not packing up a handkerchief, you know. But I'm gettin' ready to go. How am I doin' it? I'm layin' aside every weight and a sin that does so easily beset me and I'm gettin' light for the flight.

Coretta Scott King

Born April 27, 1927, in Marion, Alabama

Coretta Scott King served as president and chief executive officer of the Martin Luther King, Jr., Center for Nonviolent Social Change, Inc., in Atlanta, Georgia, for twenty-seven years. She handed over the reins to her son, Dexter Scott King, in 1995. Among the many accomplishments of her leadership was the creation of the facilities needed to house the largest archive of documents from the Civil Rights Movement, while she dedicated herself to the development of programs that train people from all over the world in Dr. King's philosophy and methods. Prior to his assassination in 1968, Mrs. King worked side by side with her husband. Since that time, she has continued in her roles as human rights leader, administrator, mother, lecturer, and newspaper columnist. She is the author of My Life with Martin Luther King, Jr. *and* The Martin Luther King, Jr., Companion, *both reprinted in 1994.*

I formed my views about life and dealing with the future at an early age. Even while I was a student at Antioch College, I took an active interest in promoting world peace, having come under the influence of Quakerism. Later, when Martin and I moved to Atlanta in 1961, I joined the Women's International League for Peace and Freedom. I was, and still am, convinced that the women of the world, united without any regard for national or racial dimensions, can become a most powerful force for international peace and brotherhood.

Martin and I were married in 1953 and the civil rights movement began in Montgomery in 1955. I remember thinking one day in Montgomery, "This is what I have been preparing for my entire life. This is the beginning of a journey. I don't know where it is going to take us, but we are involved in a worldwide struggle." It was a good feeling to know that my life had purpose and meaning. After our home in Montgomery was bombed, I had to recommit myself and my life. I realized then that I could be killed and that it was important to make this my struggle also.

Martin lifted civil rights to its broadest dimension. He often said that white people couldn't really be free until black people were free, because we are all "tied together in a bond of mutuality." He went beyond the realm of civil rights and into a more philosophical realm. Many people didn't understand his perspective at the time.

Martin had a way of making people feel important and special. It wasn't a conscious thing with him, but a natural thing. His needs and the raising of our four children were my primary concern. He knew that I was going to take care of everything at home and in this way, I was able to support him and free him so that he could go and do the work of the movement. We both felt that this was a very important contribution during this period of our lives.

But this was not the only contribution which I made to the movement. I participated in marches and rallys and spoke to women's groups and the mainstream of the peace movement. In 1964, I developed a freedom concert format initially called "The Portrait of a Nonviolent Struggle," which incorporated hymns, spirituals, and freedom songs narrating the story of the freedom struggle from Montgomery to Washington, Montgomery to Memphis, and Montgomery to Selma. The freedom concert educated and exposed the public to the history of the civil rights movement. They were also important fundraisers for the Southern Christian Leadership Conference.

Since 1968, I have concentrated my time and attention on raising my four children, developing an appropriate memorial to the life and contributions of Martin Luther King, Jr., and establishing the Martin Luther King, Jr., federal holiday. I'm also co-chair of the National Committee for Full Employment and the Full Employment Action Council.

Jewell Jackson McCabe

Born August 2, 1945, in Washington, D.C.

Behind every significant accomplishment in American society today goes a black woman, or groups of black women, unrecognized. My mission is to change that.

I grew up in a black upper-middle-class family. My father was the first black broadcaster in this country. My aunt was the first black to graduate from the Boston Conservatory of Music. We always had the biggest house on the block.

Blacks were always taught good manners. The discipline of my upbringing sheltered me. You always went to the bathroom before you left home. You were very controlled in public. You didn't use public facilities because they were not clean. You never knew they were separate. You were never subjected to those indignities.

If I am privileged, then I have a responsibility to pay back.

Black people are the only segment in American society that is defined by its weakest elements. Every other segment is defined by its highest achievement. We have to turn that around.

The majority of people on welfare are not black, brown, or yellow people. They are white people.

You factor in racism as a reality and you keep moving.

Part of the problem of upward mobility is that even when we exhibit great strengths and give good advice, we're never perceived as the person who should get the job. It's that old, boring image of always training the person that's going to be your supervisor.

When I worked for Governor Hugh Carey, I was in the Women's Division and all the women around me were white. I'd come home frustrated because I couldn't get them to make a decision. All they did was find reasons not to make decisions. I realized that white women had been so stripped of their capabilities and their self-esteem that they were not needed to be decision-makers. The difference is night and day. I am driven by a reality that I am, by hook or crook, going to make a decision.

Child care for white women is last on their agenda because it basically supplements what is first on the agenda, equal pay for equal work. Child care, however, happens to be on the top of *our* agenda, because we know we've got to work.

We are sensitive to the full range of the haves and have-nots. White women tend to see through the eyes of whatever class they come from.

Teaching dance to emotionally disturbed children was probably one of my most satisfying and wrenching experiences. Dealing with little ones from broken homes that had tried to commit suicide. I mean, how does a four-year-old try to commit suicide? And why?

The Coalition was started in 1970 by a group of twenty-four women who were quite profound and prophetic about the need to develop a contemporary forum for black women leaders. We use the volunteer corps of the Coalition to serve as role models to teach young people how to leverage resources and how to make it.

The women decided to call themselves the Coalition of 100 Black Women, hoping that they would be able to find a hundred. When I became president in 1977, we had 127. When I launched the national movement in 1981, we were 890 women in New York, and they were crying for it outside. Now we're over 6,000 in sixty-two cities.

Part of my passion with black women is that those who become achievers tend not to be involved in movements. White males tend to bond gloriously when they become accomplished. Not us. We tend to go under the rug, disappear, hide.

We've got to have a legacy of leadership. We've got to bring along with us a generation of black women who are going to confront twenty-first-century realities.

There is a confinement and a discipline and a preparation for leadership that you develop through being alone, which women are fearful of.

I do business with many corporate and political leaders. I don't think they think I can ever have the pains that other women have. You have to exude that strength in order to be respected.

It's happened several times. When I've finished speaking, someone from the audience will say, "Jewell McCabe, we've heard so much about you, but we thought you were a large, old black woman." And I remind them that I have the heart and soul of a large, old black woman.

Jewell Jackson McCabe is the past president and present chair of the National Coalition of 100 Black Women. She has worked in the public and private sectors and was appointed chairman of New York State's $205 million Jobs Training Partnership Council by Governor Mario Cuomo in 1983. Today she is president of Jewell Jackson McCabe Associates, a management consulting firm with a list of Fortune 500 clients. She is a presidential appointee to the U.S. Holocaust Memorial Council, where she is a member of the Education and Community outreach committee. McCabe serves as a member of the Board of Overseers, Wharton School of Business; the Board of Trustees of the Phelps Stokes Fund, the Board of Directors of Bard College, as well as the boards of eight additional organizations. She holds honorary doctorates from Iona College, New Rochelle, New York, and Tougaloo College, Jackson, Mississippi.

Mary Frances Berry

Born February 17, 1938, in Nashville, Tennessee

Mary Frances Berry was appointed to the United States Commission on Civil Rights by President Carter in 1980. Fired from her position by President Reagan in 1983, she successfully sued for reinstatement in Federal District Court. She has held faculty and administrative positions at several universities, and is the Geraldine R. Segal Professor of American Social Thought at the University of Pennsylvania, where she teaches history and law. Dr. Berry has received many awards and honorary degrees honoring her public service and academic activities. She has been selected by the Sienna College Research Institute and the Women's Hall of Fame as one of "America's Women of the Century." She is the author of six books, among them The Politics of Parenthood: Child Care, Women's Rights and the Myth of the Good Mother, *published in 1993, and* Black Resistance/White Law: A History of Constitutional Racism in America, *published in 1994.*

My mother always told me to be overqualified for everything. She said, "Always have more qualifications than anybody else you're sitting in the room with. If there are people there who have one degree, you get two. If they got two, you get three."

I never had any childhood really. I read my first fairy tales about three years ago.

At one point my mother had to put my brother and me in an orphanage. It was like a horror story. My mother didn't know it. They didn't feed the children properly. They'd buy rotten food from the supermarket or pick up garbage and cook it. They'd put a whole bunch of black pepper in it so you wouldn't smell that it was rotten.

My mother would give us a nickel when she came. There was a man who worked there at the place and used to sell us bones, all the children. When he knew that your mother had left you some money, he'd come and say, "If you give me that nickel, I'll give you something good to eat," and you'd buy his damn bones.

I'm not unhappy about my life. I enjoy what I do. And it's always interesting to speculate about how it would have been different. It's a sort of upbeat message I give, not "Oh, poor me. I didn't get the right food when I was little, and didn't get to read any fairy stories."

I had a high school teacher who was a wonderful woman. She took me under her wing and said, "We're going to get these rough edges off. You are a diamond in the rough. You're smart, but you've led a rather crude, backward kind of life. We're going to polish you up a bit."

I was walking down the street with my teacher in Nashville the day *Brown v. Board of Education* was decided. I saw the headline in the newspaper and I remember saying, "Look at this! This is going to be great! Starting next year the kids will all be going to school together!" And she looked at me and said, "I'm not sure it's going to happen quite next year."

I always had a job. The entire time I went to Howard and the whole time I was in graduate school at Michigan, I worked in hospital labs. Went to school full time and worked on the three-to-eleven-thirty shift full time until the day I got my PhD. They were very stressful conditions, going to school all day long, then staying up half the night to write papers while other people were going out on dates and hanging out. I mean, you need a certain amount of grit to just keep on steppin'.

I was the first woman of any race to be head of a major research university [University of Colorado at Boulder, 1976–77] in this country. It wouldn't have happened if the political and social changes had not taken place. But I had done as much or more than anybody they could compare me with—male or female, black or white.

Black people have to be sensitive in America because of our predicament. Women have to be sensitive in America because of a historical and present predicament. But poverty added on top of that is like a triple burden. It made me a more sensitive and committed person.

When it comes to the cause of justice, I take no prisoners and I don't believe in compromising.

After I was chancellor at Colorado, I went to the Department of Health, Education and Welfare and then I fought hard to get the Department of Education bill passed. And when I left—I was about forty then—I said, "Mama, I'm tired now. I think I've done enough." She said, "Oh, what are you going to do next? There's still a lot more to do."

When I did the Free South Africa protest, my mother woke up Thanksgiving morning and saw on television that I was in jail. I called her and said, "Mom, I'm in jail." And she said, "Well, it's a good cause." She didn't say, "Oh, my baby."

When you talk about America's neighborhoods, if you didn't live in America and know what country we're talking about, you could be talking about South Africa.

Housing segregation is still the major unsolved civil rights problem in America.

It's one thing to talk about helping those in the poverty situation to live better. The other thing is, how do you move people out of that generationally, and keep them out of it?

If Rosa Parks had taken a poll before she sat down in the bus in Montgomery, she'd still be standing.

In many ways what black women have contributed has been stymied. Most often the women are the ones who concoct or think of things, and the men do them. The old idea of the woman behind the man is still a very alive idea.

Race is such an ancient burden that we drag around with us in this country. It's on everybody's mind almost all the time even if they think it's not. It's part of the American psyche, to have it on your mind and to be unresolved.

Ruby Middleton Forsythe

Born June 27, 1905, in Charleston, South Carolina
Died May 28, 1992, in Charleston, South Carolina

We are laying the foundation for children to build on. I have had a few outstanding students—lawyers, ministers, and every walk of life. I had a girl that graduated from the Air Force Academy. They were poor boys and girls. They walked miles and miles to come to school, rain or shine. We tried to build in them dependability, responsibility. They appreciate that today.

You got to make them start with little things that's not in the book to teach respect.

The schoolteacher today has to be mother, father, counselor, everything. The majority of the children have nobody to sit down with them and teach them the little things that are right from the things that are wrong. Sometimes I have to stop the class, close the book, and sit down and say, "Let's talk." Because their parents just don't have time.

A few children come new, you know, and don't know the rules and regulations. And my children say, "Miss Ruby, that boy over there cuss just now." I say, "Bring that boy in to me." I got a little mixture here that I keep in a bottle and I put it in their mouth and make them hold it there until it starts bubbling. It's nothing but peroxide, Listerine, and water, but they think they're going to die. That peroxide starts working with that water and then all these white bubbles start coming down and I won't let them spit it out. They start crying right off as soon as they see me gettin' the bottle. That'll cure all bad language.

For discipline I let the parents know I am not going to kill the children, but I am not going to put up with their foolishness. And if they don't want that, then don't enroll them in this school.

I tell my children. Never use the words, "I can't." Say, "I'll try." I tell them, "Now God has given us something up in the head, and you know why He put it there? Because He wants you to use it. If you don't use it He is going to take it away and give it to the next boy or girl."

When they bring their big bags to school, I say, "Leave your pocketbook at home." I say, "When you fill up your head, then the head will help you to fill up your pocketbook."

I am not against computers, but I am against putting them in a class or giving them to children when they have not laid a foundation to depend upon themselves. Develop that mind first.

I say leadership is good when you don't overstep it, if you can lead and then be able to follow at times. We have quite a few people who are able to lead, but they can't follow. That's why I say it's good for a child to lose as well as win. They must learn in life they are going to be up today and maybe down tomorrow.

I do not like forced integration. I may be wrong. I do not like forced anything. Understand, as a youngster I lived in a white neighborhood with a white neighbor next door. We would go to them, they would go to us. If they had anything, we had it. We lived just like one. We didn't think about no integration.

Quaker missionaries set up a school in Charleston for black children, Avery Institute. And then Ashley Hall was set up for the whites. The two schools weren't integrated but the same courses that they studied at Ashley Hall, we got at Avery Institute. Everybody and anybody was not accepted. They had to know something of your background or something about your people before you could be recommended. It was one of the most cultural things that we had in Charleston.

We have some good white teachers and they are concerned about black children learning. And we have some good black teachers. On both sides, it's the same way. But we have some teachers who are in the classroom only for the check.

We've had the Ku Klux Klan march all through. If you see the type person that's into those marches, you can tell they don't feel good about themselves. They are insecure. They don't feel that they will ever reach the height of some of their own people. And then they feel that some of the blacks will suppress them or surpass them in a way and that the opportunity some have they can't get. So all that works on them.

When I see my product leave and accomplish something worthwhile, then it gives me the urge to try to do a little bit more for a few more. I see the need of these children today. That's the only reason I am holding on, but I don't know how much longer I'm gonna hold on.

Miss Ruby, a teacher for over sixty years, taught in a one-room schoolhouse on Pawleys Island, South Carolina for half a century. She summoned her students, who ranged from preschoolers to fourth graders, with an old-fashioned brass hand bell, a gift from her first class in 1939. Her school, the Holy Cross-Faith Memorial School, was supported by the Episcopal Church and maintained by the students' parents, many of whom were alumni themselves. In 1987, a national newsmagazine featured her in a salute to "Everyday Heroes."

Jean Blackwell Hutson

Born September 7, 1914, in Summerfield, Florida
Died February 4, 1998 in New York City, New York

I was born three months premature. My father was about to knock up this little wooden box to bury me in, so he told me. He could hardly hit the nails, he was crying so hard. Then I started yelling and I've been talking ever since.

In 1936, I received a telegram to come here to work at the old 135th Street branch library. I was substituting for the librarian of the Schomburg Collection, which was on the top floor, while she was out on maternity leave. In my freshness I got into trouble with Mr. Schomburg.

His books had been catalogued by the Dewey Decimal System, but he had ignored that and he kept the books in his rarest collection arranged by the height of their spine and their hue. So one night I stayed and arranged these books by the decimal system so that everybody else could locate them from the card catalogue. When he came in the next day, he couldn't find anything. He forbade me to come back into the place. We had had an amiable relationship until then.

He was a very cordial, loquacious, arty person to know. He often said that he was inspired by bad teaching. He and some other dark-skinned boys in his native Puerto Rico had asked why they didn't study Negro history and they were told that Negroes had no history. I think that's when he started collecting every evidence he could find on Negroes.

Schomburg had a different concept of our history. His collection included nonbook materials, because he found many African art objects more revealing of African history than books. Schomburg's library was one that incorporated the idea of Negroes in the other parts of the world as well as the United States, whereas the other collections all started with slavery, as if this was the beginning. This collection was purchased by the New York Public Library in 1926, and it became the center of all sorts of meetings.

During the Harlem Renaissance people came from the Caribbean as well as from the South and brought together all this inspiration and protest. Léopold Sédar Senghor, the African scholar [and long-time president of Senegal], feels that art and literature are the precursors of political activity. He said that the Harlem Renaissance inspired the political independence movements of Africa. Every last one of them first had the writing and the musical expression before the political explosion.

After I left the Schomburg Collection I became the guinea pig to go and work in other branch libraries where, supposedly, no Negroes could work. I learned that customers really didn't care what color handed them the books, unless you didn't find what they wanted. Then they might look at you and call you a nigger. But they didn't care that much.

I was at the Harlem Library and that was when Langston [Hughes] and Ralph [Ellison] and the boys used to come and sit in the library and talk. That's where I first knew John Henrik Clark and I met Richard Wright that way.

It took me ten years to return as curator of the Schomburg. When the Schomburg Collection was transferred from the branch libraries to the research libraries [in 1972 and renamed the Schomburg Center for Research in Black Culture], I remember one man said that the branch libraries loved people and the research libraries loved books.

I cleaned out a storehouse of uncatalogued materials, four closets of stuff. We got all that material catalogued. Some of it was fabulous. There was a WPA [Works Progress Administration] art project on Negroes in the history of New York.

Kwame Nkrumah [then the president of Ghana] sent a very eloquent letter for W.E.B. Du Bois's ninetieth birthday in which he paid tribute to what the Schomburg had meant to him. That was where he got a chance to read his own history. He wanted this kind of library for his young people.

That was how I went to work at the Africana collection at the University of Ghana in the 1964–65 semester. It was really a very liberating experience for me. I remember feeling ashamed of being fifty years old, an old lady. But being in Africa meant that I was respected and sought after. I really was surprised how at home I felt and liberated. And then I realized that it was my first experience being accepted as a person without regard to race.

One of the most rewarding experiences I had was opening up the Africana collection. It was very good, but it was limited to people who lived and stayed on the African continent. One day I just couldn't stand it. I went in and had a three-hour session with the head librarian, an Englishman who had worked all his life on the African continent. He finally conceded that those of us who lived abroad were still Africans, that we were still making our contribution to the continent and still had a place in the African collection. I was proud that I left that collection with historical and geographical boundaries greatly extended.

One of the main things the Schomburg does is supply the ammunition for change. It is a part of the public library, open to everybody, everywhere. You don't have to be registered at the university to have access to the materials. You don't have to pay an admission fee to come in, and the catalogue is available all around the world. That has been and continues to be the opportunity that the Schomburg offers.

For thirty-two years, Jean Blackwell Hutson guided the development of the Schomburg Center for Research in Black Culture, the world's most comprehensive collection of materials documenting the history and culture of peoples of African descent. From curator in 1948 to chief until 1980, she worked to acquire, catalogue, and exhibit materials under the auspices of the New York Public Library. She lectured on history at the City College of New York for over a decade and retired in 1984.

Anna Arnold Hedgeman

Born July 5, 1899, in Marshalltown, Iowa
Died January 17, 1990, in New York City, New York

Dr. Anna Arnold Hedgeman, a spirited activist and politician, was the first woman to serve in the cabinet of a mayor of New York. Her role as a member of the cabinet of Mayor Robert Wagner from 1954 to 1958 was preceded and followed by work with governmental and civic organizations, both national and international. As Coordinator of Special Projects for the Commission on Religion and Race of the National Council of Churches, she was the only woman to serve on the administrative committee under the ten co-chairmen who called for the March on Washington in 1963. She is credited with recruiting 40,000 Protestant churchmen to participate. In 1965, The Trumpet Sounds, an autobiographical work, was published. This volume tells the story of a woman of African heritage struggling to fulfill the goals of our Constitution.

I'm my father's daughter. I'm a product of 1865 as well as 1900. He had come out of the slave system. His mother and father had been slaves and they were in our household in Saint Paul, Minnesota.

At breakfast time we had prayers for the day and they were in quite specific terms because at night you reported on how you had been useful. *Useful* was always the word, useful to yourself, and useful to life.

My father taught me that I would understand education better from the South than any place else. [After graduating from Hamline University in Saint Paul, and planning to teach,] I chose Mississippi because they said it was the worst of the system. I wanted to start off with whatever was worst and see what I could do. In a very short time, I was indoctrinated. I never saw more eager teachers and students. Education was continuous.

If we had in this country right now the fundamental quality of education that the Negro college in the South had, we wouldn't be in the mess we're in.

In Mississippi everything was off limits. After two years' experience I knew that in my lifetime I would never know normal freedom. And I never have. . . .

We're neither free nor very brave. That doesn't mean that individuals aren't. But as a nation.

The workers taught me themselves. This laundry worker was in a club of mine, the YWCA, which was the pioneering organization at that time. They would work out their program and then they wouldn't carry it out. And so one night, I stopped 'em, "I'm tired of sitting with you as you plan a program and then you do not follow through." A woman stopped afterward and asked me, "Have you ever worked in a laundry?" I said, "No."

So by innocence and ignorance—and it's both—I went through the whole process of working in the laundry and at the end of the week, I didn't want any program you'd help cook up in a YWCA. I only wanted a bed.

Eleanor Roosevelt was the first unelected woman president of these United States. When the war came, the Negro nurse had a awful time getting into the whole thing to take care of her men whom the others were not going to take care of. It was known that that was true. We were worried and I wanted to see Mrs. Roosevelt. I sat in the second row where she was speaking and then I made myself last in the receiving line. I had my sentence ready. "Mrs. Roosevelt, the Negro nurse is being cheated by our government in terms of the war effort, and I need to talk with you." She looked at me and said, "Of course," and invited the organizers for tea at her apartment. Believe it or not, within two weeks things began to happen. She knew people.

My husband never let the fact that I was a woman fail to make him encourage me where he thought I was right, criticize me where I wasn't. We came out of the same quality of family.

He was a concert artist with a gorgeous voice, lyric tenor, and he couldn't even get an audition in this town [New York]. One night I came home and found a note from him that said, "I quit the Cotton Club tonight. I couldn't sing my songs in a strange land." Rejection of the best was the order of the day.

Look how we sacrificed Martin Luther King. He taught non-violence in the midst of the war of Montgomery. Do you hear me? And then did the audacious thing—asked us to come out of Vietnam.

His dream was for democracy. I sat on the stage with him as he made that speech and I almost died. Because he was young, he was able to articulate beautifully, and he cared. And here he was being misused. He was being used to claim that we had a democracy.

White people have suffered as much as we have. They just don't know it because they got the money, at least, and the so-called prestige of professionals.

I hate the word *liberal*. Liberal with what and for whom?

Johnnie Tillmon

Born April 10, 1926, in Scott, Arkansas
Died November 22, 1995, in Los Angeles, California

Johnnie Tillmon-Blackston was founding chairperson and, in 1972, became the director of the National Welfare Rights Organization. Her firsthand experience as a "welfare mother," combined with a talent for mobilizing people and resources, helped bring attention to the multi-layered inequities of the welfare system. From her home in Watts, she traveled to more than 800 cities, organizing people around social and political issues.

Marriage and raising kids was not my idea of a life. My idea was to go places, to travel. I used to dream about the trains. I never dreamed about the husband and the pitter-patter of little feet in the house, and the white picket fence. That wasn't in my dreams at all.

My break came when I went to California, the land of sunshine and smog, in 1960. I had six children. I went to work as a shirt line operator. I could do 120 dress shirts an hour, 150 work shirts an hour, the front and back of them.

When I moved over here in the housing project, I joined in with this organization beautifying the community and helping people who needed help. After I got sick and ended up in the hospital, the president of the organization and the secretary came to my house and said, "Tillmon, we understand that you are sick." I said, "Yeah, but I'll be going back to work soon." They said, "We also understand that your oldest daughter has been cutting classes." I didn't know that. She was in junior high school. He said, "We also understand that your baby lives elsewhere 'cause you don't have nobody to keep it." I said, "That's right." He said, "Well, we're going to get you on welfare." I said, "No, no, no. I don't want to go on no welfare."

I had heard talk about these people on welfare, that women were on welfare to have babies. They talked about how lazy women were, how shiftless. I've never been lazy. I was still protesting, but I signed my name and said, "We'll try it."

I got this idea of organizing women on welfare who lived in the project. After interviewing three hundred women, we had only one say that she was perfectly satisfied being on welfare. One woman.

We stopped a lot of harassment and then we got involved in the state politics of the welfare program. There used to be a time when they would look in your dirty clothes hamper for men's clothes. They used to come to your house at midnight and they used to pump the kids, "Where's your daddy?"

If your kids look clean or your house looks clean, then you must be doing something fraudulent, because they understand that you really shouldn't be able to do what you do with the money you get. So when you trade *a* man for *the* man, you still got somebody telling you how to live your life.

Black social workers are just as bad as white social workers when it comes to making you feel that they're giving you the money out of their pockets. I don't know what their problem is 'cause I tell them all off, but that's just me. You raise hell with the social worker, who you don't need to raise hell with, 'cause she doesn't know much more than you do.

What's really bad about welfare is attitudes. People still don't understand what welfare is for. We grew to learn that it didn't start with the social workers; it was above them. You go on to your elected officials, your governor, your senator, your president. That's where the problem is. They set up there on their behinds and make decisions on how much money a person should live off of. But their whiskey tabs are more than what they decide for a poor person to live off.

Everybody makes money off of welfare. If nobody ever went to apply for aid, your social workers, your specialists, your directors and administrators, all those kind of folks wouldn't have a job.

Everybody benefits from that money. We get medical cards. Who benefits from that? The doctors, the pharmacists, and the drugstores. They depend on it. They got their own business budgeted around 1st and 15th money.

I will never accept that I got a free ride. It wasn't free at all. My ancestors were brought here against their will. They were made to work and help build this country. I worked in the cotton fields from the age of seven. I worked in the laundry for twenty-three years. I worked for the national organization for nine years. I just retired from city government after twelve-and-a-half years.

There's six white women to every black one on AFDC [Aid to Families with Dependent Children] in this country. But nobody never talks about that. I met a group of white women from Kentucky who said, "You cannot leave us out of this organization. Because we are white does not mean that we are free. We're having the same problem with our welfare department that you have as a black woman." So that's why the organization was made up out of everybody. You will find aplenty white people who are poor and on welfare, who are not able to get out from slave bondage.

I was forty-six years old and in the nation's capital before I was ever called a nigger. I politely took off my coat, handed my bag to my attorney, and went and had me a fist city on the man's head. He didn't hit me back or nothin', but he ran. Never had been called that by a white person out of all the thirty-five years I lived in Little Rock and Arkansas. But many years ago I had decided that's what I was going to do.

If I was the President of the United States, I would provide more jobs. There are a lot of people that would love to work that are either underqualified or overqualified. I don't want you giving me nothing. You just put it out there, I'll get it myself. A lot of people would get it themselves.

I believe in rhetoric to a certain extent. But you can only rhetoricize so long and then you have to deal with fact. Now, I can do as much rhetoricizing as the next person. But sometimes I had to start a mess to get to the facts.

Myrlie Evers

Born March 1, 1933, in Vicksburg, Mississippi

In 1987, Myrlie Evers became the first black woman to be appointed Commissioner to the Board of Public Works in Los Angeles. She is the widow of Medgar Evers, who was field secretary for the NAACP in Mississippi from 1954 until his assassination in 1963. Her book, For Us the Living, *tells the story of her husband and the Civil Rights Movement. In 1994, a jury convicted the killer of Medgar Evers; it had taken thirty-one years for Myrlie Evers (now Evers-Williams) to reach closure. She donated the Evers family home in Jackson, Mississippi to Tougaloo College, where it serves as the Medgar Evers Center. In 1995, Evers-Williams was elected chairperson of the NAACP and continued to serve until 1998. That year, at the NAACP's annual convention, Coretta Scott King presented her with the Springarn Medal, its highest award. Thirty-six years before, she had accepted the award on behalf of the slain Medgar. Today, Evers-Williams oversees the Medgar Evers Center at Tougaloo College and directs MEW Associated, Inc., a consulting firm.*

I married Medgar at the age of eighteen. He was a wordly veteran of World War II. He often joked that he not only married me because he loved me, but also because I was young, inexperienced, and talented, and he could mold me into the kind of woman that he wanted. I resented that. Medgar would have been very dissatisfied with a subservient wife. Therein lay the contradiction. He not only wanted someone who was actively involved, who was an achiever, but who was also the traditional woman as well.

Medgar knew that the course he had chosen might cause him to lose his life. Those who were threatened by him labeled him irrational, a fool, a young upstart, all because he had a vision that was beyond what most people could even imagine. There was an urgency in almost everything that he did. He was never mine, totally. He belonged to his people, the struggle, and his country. In a way, Medgar constantly prepared me not only to survive but to be able to live and achieve without him. He believed in me and my abilities, even at a time when I questioned my skills. I appreciated that.

If one were to take the map of Mississippi and then take the list of people who were killed, beaten, lynched, raped, and who lost homes during the fifties and sixties, and placed red pins for each incident, the state would be a red mass of suffering and pain.

Medgar was killed June 12, 1963. President Kennedy was killed in November of the same year. I was touring the country at that time and remember saying that if people like Medgar are killed because of their fight for justice and freedom, then anyone, including the President, could suffer the same fate. When President Kennedy was killed, I felt the anguish once again. It was like a nightmare repeated.

In the barrel of racism, Mississippi was at the bottom. I was born there, lived there most of my life, bore my children there, and lost my husband there. I know hatred. I know the bitterness that can envelop body and soul. I know what it is like to be in court and watch the man accused of murdering your husband and witness the Governor of Mississippi walk in, sit down, shake hands and proudly slap the accused man on the back. You know it when the accused stands before the media and says that he is glad that he got rid of varmints.

The first year after Medgar's death, my fuel for survival was hatred. Living in the same house was too hard. Every time I walked out the door, I saw his blood—the place where he had been shot down. I had to move from Mississippi so that my children and I could start anew. We left a year and a month after Medgar's death and moved to California where I worked part time and went to college part time. We have benefited so much from what he gave. But it still does not fill that emptiness in our hearts. I will always miss Medgar.

I am still restless. I miss what we had during that time. A sense of purpose, people coming together, meeting the challenges head on, a kind of solidarity that you don't find any more. The gains that we have made are slowly but surely slipping away from us. I feel as though I should shout from mountain tops to valleys, ''Don't you see what's happening? Don't let history repeat itself!''

I see the same challenges of the past with us, maybe cloaked a little differently. We are still plagued with racism. We still find discrimination in the job market, in education, and housing. There are still covenants to keep minorities out of certain geographical areas. I have faced discrimination, not only due to the color of my skin, but because I am female. I have had jobs that have been the same or equivalent to jobs of white males and have received anywhere from 15 to 30 percent less pay.

But we keep a-coming. Strong as we've always been, more aware of ourselves, our strength, and power potential, willing to take more risks. I don't see a massive number of black women involved in the women's movement, but I see a growth of black women's organizations that are addressing not only politics, but other survival issues that face us.

I was very fortunate to have married Walter E. Williams, a man who is my very best friend, a man who is strong enough to have allowed me to have mourned Medgar for years, a man who is interested in keeping Medgar's memory and deeds alive as best we can. There are almost no books on Medgar. Material is very limited in libraries, in schools. We hope to change that.

It has been in many ways a painful growth, but it has been absolutely marvelous. I have reached a point in my life where I understand the pain and the challenges, and my attitude is one of standing up with open arms to meet all of them.

Faye Wattleton

Born July 8, 1943, in Saint Louis, Missouri

Although I came from a poor and humble background, I did not come from a family of people who had a poverty view of the world. I came from people who viewed the world as attainable.

Traveling through the South in the summer, it was a rule that before you bought gas you asked the service station attendant whether they had bathroom facilities for blacks. If they said no, we drove on. It was my parents' way of protesting the system economically. We're talking about the fifties, pre-Martin Luther King days. Once, outside New Orleans, I remember my father asking the usual question and I found that there was only an open hole in the ground. My father protested and said, "We're not dogs. Stop pumping the gas." In Algiers, Louisiana, that could have been reason for lynching. But it never occurred to him that he should do anything else. So I grew up in a family of people who lived their politics more than they proselytized their politics.

My mother felt that I should be a missionary nurse. Her dream for me was to go abroad to Africa and other parts of the world to serve the suffering. I have been something of a disappointment to her ideal, but I think, from my own view, I have done missionary work nonetheless.

I had the experience of taking care of a seventeen-year-old girl who died as a result of an instillation of bleach and Lysol that she and her mother had concocted to end her pregnancy. That was a very dramatic experience. You're looking at a healthy, beautiful human being who just dies because of the poison. That was the closest I had come to the desperation that women feel.

Roe v. Wade opened the final gate of liberation for women. It took women out of the bondage of their reproductive organs. To be able to take control of their reproductive lives was perhaps more liberating than any other advancement that women have achieved.

What bothers me today is that a lot of young women do not know the circumstances and conditions that existed in those years. Without an understanding, I'm afraid that we may see apathy develop, that people will simply take it for granted.

I know of no women who think it's a great idea to have an abortion. That represents a fundamental misunderstanding about what women go through in managing their fertility.

If those who oppose abortion care about the living as much as they care about those who are not with us and only have the potential for being with us, why are so many nonwhite children unadopted? No one is breaking down the door to take them in.

Because of AIDS, the conversation at least has been opened to talk about sex, but we will only talk about it around disease and death. We still have a great deal of difficulty talking about it as a part of normal human behavior.

It's irrational that we are so uptight and so scared about morals that we'd rather see little girls in the street pregnant than prevent that condition. It's a manifestation of our fundamental conflicts about sex.

I happened to turn on a television show and the discussion at nine in the morning was about things that turn us on sexually and what we like to do in foreplay. Please, don't misunderstand me, I'm not shocked by this discussion. What I'm saying is that we can have this kind of explicit discussion at nine in the morning and then network officials will piously say to us, "Oh, we can't advertise birth control products because it's controversial and people will be offended."

I want the same thing for blacks, Hispanics, and whites that I want for myself and my child. And that is the ability to take charge of our lives and not be victimized by reproduction.

Faye Wattleton served as president of Planned Parenthood Federation of America from 1978 to 1992. She was the first woman to head the nation's largest family planning agency. Today, she remains a determined advocate of reproductive rights and responsibilities. As co-founder, president, and CEO of the Center for Gender Equality, Wattleton designed this not-for-profit research and education institute to support efforts to eliminate persistent barriers to full equality. Wattleton holds thirteen honorary degrees among her numerous awards, which include the Jefferson Award for Greatest Public Service Performed by Private Citizen and the Margaret Sanger Award, PFFA. She is a member of the National Women's Hall of Fame. Her book, Life on the Line, *is an autobiography skillfully woven with a historical account of the Reproductive Rights Movement.*

Faye Wattleton with her daughter, Felicia Gordon, now twenty-three years old, and a graduate of Harvard University, Magna cum Laude, Phi Beta Kappa.

Angela Yvonne Davis

Born January 26, 1944, in Birmingham, Alabama

I grew up in a neighborhood in Birmingham that came to be called Dynamite Hill, because whenever a black family moved into a house on the other side of the border separating the black neighborhood from the white neighborhood, there would be a bombing or the house would be burned down.

When I was a child we developed games that were—when I think back on them—an instinctive resistance to the system. We would dare each other to run across the street, or to run up on the porches of the white people, or ring their doorbells and then try to get back to our side before they came out.

I was very fortunate to grow up in a family with a history of activist involvement. My mother and father had been involved in the NAACP, the Southern Negro Youth Congress, and the Scottsboro Nine. As a child I was told that the system was irrational.

It is important not only to have the awareness and to feel impelled to become involved, it's important that there be a forum out there to which one can relate, an organization, a movement.

I joined the Communist party because I felt the need to relate the struggle for the liberation of black people to the working-class struggles of people of all racial backgrounds.

There was a period during which there was a concerted ideological attack on black women. The Moynihan Report had been released in 1965. Someone from the national office of SNCC [Student Nonviolent Coordinating Committee] did not like the idea that there were so many women in the leadership of SNCC and decided to restructure the organization. Some of the men went along with it, not all of them, and some of the women agreed that they should step back, so it was really not a male versus female situation. That struggle, that internal struggle actually destroyed the organization.

People were simply articulating these ideas, not knowing the origin, and not recognizing the extent to which they constituted a conscious effort to create confusion within the movement.

It was just assumed, of anybody who was active during that era of the black movement, that you were going to be hateful and antiwhite. But I've never been that way. I've been pretty much the way I am now. I noticed for a while that there were never any pictures of me that showed me with my mouth closed. I always had my mouth open, so people who saw those images were under the impression that I was always screaming and hollering.

It didn't occur to me when I was fired from my position at UCLA that I would not fight. That just was not a possibility.

There was a statute dating from the McCarthy era still on the books which said that the University of California would not hire any members of the Communist party. I eventually had that eradicated by taking the case up to the Supreme Court.

It came as a real shock to me that I was targeted by the same forces I had been challenging. It was very, very scary. I didn't know what was going to happen to me. I knew that I didn't want to turn myself in because I didn't think that I could get a fair trial. I might not even make it to the courtroom if I surrendered. When I was finally captured, it was sort of a relief. Finally, you do have some grasp of what's going to be happening the next day.

I was feeling very down, very depressed. They put me in a cell that night, and I could hear people chanting outside of the prison, "Free Angela Davis." From that very first night until the last day of my trial, I got a great deal of my strength from people out there fighting for me.

All my family were very supportive during the time I was in jail. My mother traveled, my father spoke. My brother, a professional football player at that time, received a letter from the president, who was a fan. He sympathized with my brother that he had a sister who was a crazy Communist.

Black women have had to develop a larger vision of our society than perhaps any other group. They have had to understand white men, white women, and black men. And they have had to understand themselves. When black women win victories, it is a boost for virtually every segment of this society.

The women's movement as it exists today would not be what it is had it not been for the movement for black liberation.

Black women have had the burden or the privilege of being spokespersons for all the oppressed in this society. And sometimes, of course, black women have just argued for the right to be tired.

I never really sought to be a public figure. But that was my historical fate, that was a challenge. As much as it seemed to be totally incongruous with my personality, I had to attempt to accept that challenge. During critical periods of my life, I never hesitated to do what I did.

I will never cease to criticize the judicial system for the cavalier way they argue that once a person is found not guilty, that is a vindication of that person and an indication that the system works.

Angela Davis was one of the most publicized political activists of the 1960s and 1970s. The subject of a nationwide police hunt after she was implicated in the 1970 Soledad Brothers shooting, she was imprisoned, tried, and acquitted in 1972. Her autobiography was published in 1974. Other books include Women, Race and Class *(1982);* Women, Culture and Politics *(1989); and* Blues Legacies and Black Feminism *(1998). She is a tenured professor with the History of Consciousness Department of the University of California at Santa Cruz. In 1995, she was awarded a Presidential Chair for a three-year project to increase feminist and ethnic studies at the school. Davis remains politically active: jailed for almost two years while awaiting trial, she is keenly aware of the plight of incarcerated women, and is one of the world's most outspoken prison abolitionists.*

Betty Shabazz

Born May 28, 1940, in Detroit, Michigan
Died June 23, 1997, New York City, New York

Dr. Betty Shabazz served on the faculty of Medgar Evers College of the City University of New York from 1976; she was the school's director of communications and public relations at the time of her death. After the assassination in 1965 of her husband, El-Hajj Malik El-Shabazz, better known as Malcolm X, she earned a master's degree in health administration and then a doctorate in higher education administration and curriculum development from the University of Massachusetts at Amherst. She also hosted a radio program, "A Forum for Women," in New York City.

The first severe reality? When I left Detroit to go to college in the South, my mother was at the train station. She was trying to mumble something. Whatever she was trying to tell me, she was not very good at it, and I laughed to myself. She was a bundle of confidence and here she was just tripping over her words. But the minute I got off that train, I knew what she was trying to say. She was trying to tell me in ten words or less about racism.

I met Malcolm at the mosque on 116th Street in New York when I was a nursing student. A nurse's aide invited me to her house for dinner. It was our custom to eat the tasteless, waterlogged, unattractive hospital food. Afterward we went to the mosque to hear someone present a paper. My friend asked, "Did you enjoy yourself? Why didn't you join?" I said, "I was not under the impression that you brought me here to join. Besides, my mother would kill me, and additionally I don't even understand the philosophy." My family were Methodists and I had decided at the age of thirteen I was going to die a Methodist.

She said, "I want you to meet our minister. He is handsome, disciplined, and very smart, and all of the sisters like him." And so I finally met this guy.

Malcolm was the first adult that I met who helped me face the discrimination I experienced in the South. Everyone else, including my parents, didn't want to discuss it. It was like bad manners to discuss it. It didn't exist, and if you didn't talk about it, it would go away. I wanted to go back to be able to talk to him.

He was all-giving, all-helping, and it didn't look like anybody was helping him. He needed care. He worked very hard. He was a workaholic. And I was thinking that maybe I was the person to help him.

He is the one person during my lifetime that I am delighted to have known. When I think in terms of leadership, I measure people by his yardstick. Some people don't make a connection between what they say and how they live. He understood himself. He felt that he had value. He loved his parents. He loved his people, and later he loved me with the same passion.

Malcolm was on time. He was totally correct. They attempted to promote him as a violent person, a hater of whites. He was a sensitive man, a very understanding person and yes, he disliked the behavior of some whites. One needs only to examine history and analyze the present condition of the

African diaspora to justify his conceptual framework. He had a reality-based agenda. Most people can't deal with reality, but indulge heavily in fantasy and fear.

Some leaders felt that Malcolm had no business in Africa, that the African problem was not our problem, that he should be in Mississippi and Alabama. He believed in and supported civil rights efforts, but he felt that we must elevate the struggle to one of human rights where we would get more support and sweeping changes, thereby improving the quality of life for the African diaspora significantly.

Some of the same people who criticized him would call the house or come by and say, "You're right, absolutely right, but we would get nowhere if you were not out there."

I made an unrealistic decision after Malcolm was assassinated. I said I would never mingle again with society, because I thought there was so much injustice in the world. However, it is impossible to create an environment for children to grow in and develop in isolation. It is imperative that one mix in society on some level and at some time.

Malcolm helped me deal with my own internal strength. He would sometimes say, "Girl, when I die, don't cry, because the salt from your tears will make you bitter. Remember Lot's wife?" One cannot be bitter because you block your own progress.

On my radio program I deal with topics I think young people or people who are trying to find their way might enjoy. I might talk about new career openings or options for women who find themselves in positions where they must make decisions for themselves and their families on whatever level.

When I was doing my research for my dissertation, I studied a group of people from 45 independent African states who met quarterly. Once they would not have spoken to someone because they were of a different tribe or educational level. Some were Moslem, some were Christian, some believed in the indigenous religions, some were Hindus, et cetera. What was really revolutionary was that leaders representing different countries sat in the same room together at the same conference table, improving the quality of life of their people, making decisions where the majority vote would be accepted and implemented.

We can say "Peace on Earth," we can sing about it, preach about it, or pray about it, but if we have not internalized the mythology to make it happen inside of us, then it will not be.

Queen Mother Audley Moore

Born July 27, 1898, in New Iberia, Louisiana
Died, May 2, 1997, New York City, New York

I was about nineteen or twenty when Marcus Garvey came to New Orleans and the mayor wouldn't allow him to speak. Although the hall was full of people, we all had to go home. We were so incensed, we decided to demand that he speak. So the next night, everybody came to the hall again, and we were told to bring our piece with us. Everybody went with a gun. I had two, one in my bosom and one in my pocketbook.

The hall was packed with people but it was also packed with police officers, all white. When Garvey came in we were so happy. Garvey said, "My friends, I want to apologize for not being able to speak to you last night, but the mayor of New Orleans was used as a stooge by the police department to prevent me from speaking." The police jumped up and said, "I'll run you in for that." And when he said that, everybody took their piece out, held it up in the air, stood on the benches, and said, "Speak, Garvey, speak."

Garvey said, "As I was saying . . ." And the police turned red as crawfish and filed out of there like little wounded puppy dogs.

Marcus Garvey was a great man. He made us understand about Africa, what it meant and the great heritage we had.

I went to Los Angeles in the twenties because they said that everybody was free there. But the people there said, "We got it bad here. If you're looking for freedom, you should go to Chicago." I went to Chicago and found out that people were living worse than they were living in New Orleans. Then they said, "Oh no, you should go to Harlem." So I came to Harlem and found conditions just as bad. In Harlem, they had For Whites Only signs in the windows. Big signs, child, in Harlem.

So there wasn't nothing to do but get into the struggle.

I tried to organize the domestic workers. The white women would go up to the place in the Bronx where the black women gathered. They'd look up their dresses and look at their knees. If they had crust on their knees, they'd hire them. If they didn't have crust on their knees, they wouldn't hire them. For fifteen cents an hour. It was just like slavery time.

About 1931 I signed up for the International Labor Defense and then I became a Communist. The party called for separation of the states. They wanted us to have a black republic and that sounded good. Some years later it changed; then the Communists said that we wanted integration and they put down the black republic. I left the party. I thought we were on our own and we'd get ourselves together. I don't see any other way.

Negro is a terrible word. I am responsible for our people putting down that word. I'm opposed to *black*, too. Neither one indicates where you come from and both of them are used derogatorily.

They not only called us Negroes, they made us Negroes, things that don't know where they came from and don't even care that they don't know. Negro is a state of mind and they massacred our minds.

When they decided to use *black* in the Black Power Conference, I fought that because it didn't indicate that we came from any place at all. It was always used to indicate things that were bad.

I thought that we should use *Africans*. We're African people.

I met Malcolm X during an open-air meeting. We became friends. Malcolm told me he couldn't talk about Africa because [the leader of the Nation of Islam] Elijah Muhammad wasn't talking about Africa. Elijah didn't want to hear nothing about Africa. "What did the Africans ever do for us?" he said to me. Those were his exact words.

I went to Dr. Kwame Nkrumah's funeral. That was the first time I had been to Africa. When the ship landed, I cried, I cried, I cried. I felt the lash on the backs of my people. Just looking at the land, it looked like it had been there forever. I thought, "Lord, look what they've robbed us of. I don't even know my people. They're talking but I don't understand them." Everything just came down on me. I never cried so much in my life. They wanted me to stay, gave me a house and everything. But my struggle is right here.

Ever since 1950, I've been on the trail fighting for reparations. They owe us more than they could ever pay. They stole our language, they stole our culture. They stole us from our mothers and fathers and took our names away from us. They worked us free of charge eighteen hours a day, seven days a week, under the lash, for centuries. We lost over 100 million lives in the traffic of slavery.

It's past due. The United States will never be able to pay us all they owe us. They don't have the money. But they'll owe it. They've got to do it, to save white America, they've got to do it. I'll be able to rest when we get reparations.

Do you know the Africans have European names? It's a big job teaching Africans to put down those names and take up their own name. I'm Queen Mother Moore. The Moors were a great African nation, you know, so I kept my name.

Queen Mother Moore dedicated her life to active struggle on behalf of all people of African heritage. She organized on many fronts, from the great influenza epidemic of 1918 in Muscle Shoals, Alabama, where she worked as a volunteer nurse, to the United Nations, where she presented petitions in the late 1950s charging genocide and demanding reparations to descendants of former slaves. The founder and former president of the Universal Association of Ethiopian Women, she was a life member of both the Universal Negro Improvement Association and the National Council of Negro Women.

Harriet Elizabeth Byrd

Born April 20, 1926, in Cheyenne, Wyoming

My dad was the first black child born in Laramie, Wyoming. There are four generations of my family in the state of Wyoming. There was so much land, so much for everyone here. I think that both the whites and the blacks respected each other, because this was a hard climate to live in. If you could come to Wyoming and make it through the winters, they didn't care what color you were.

We've had black mountain men. Beckworth's Pass is named after a black mountain man. There is a great history of the black cowboy in this territory. Many of them were runaway slaves. This was a good place to hide.

This is where they had the buffalo soldiers. The Indians were quite confused about blacks in Arizona and in the Dakota Territory here. They called them buffalo soldiers because of their curly hair and the color of their skin. When they had Indian uprisings sometimes, they would send the black soldiers in, and that was confusing to the Indians, too.

They had the cavalry here. When they brought the military here at Warren Air Force Base, they had segregated the troops. And that's where segregation came from. It started with the cavalry. Wherever they had military in Wyoming, that's where you saw segregation.

In our community here, we still have a great turnover of

in a little mayonnaise jar. I shook it up and down and I pulled out West Virginia.

President Davis of West Virginia State College wrote me a beautiful letter, and the registrar also put a little note in there. They said. ''We've never had a student from the state of Wyoming and we would like to have you.''

That's the first time I was ever away from home, the first time I had been in a black environment. Being at that black college did a whole lot for me. It gave me respect for myself.

When I graduated from college I thought I could run back here and get a job. When I went before the board of the Department of Education, they said they didn't hire minorities.

Public school teachers were not degreed in the state at that time. But I had a Bachelor of Science in Education. I was more qualified to teach than most of them that were teaching. Ten years later I got the job. I was the first black full-time teacher they had.

Little children don't really care about the color of your skin that much. When you see children playing in the playground, all they're interested in is learning and getting along.

My dad taught all of us there's more to life than just complaining. The reason I ran was because of my dad. We talked all the time about everything. I was teaching school and I said, ''Lawyers don't have to worry about money, but why teachers?'' My dad said to me, ''There you go! If you really want teachers to have an increase in salary, you ought to run for the legislature.'' And he reached down in his pocket and said, ''Here's your filing fee.''

My husband [James W. Byrd] has a lot to do with why I got elected. He was chief of police under eight mayors in Cheyenne. He was the first black chief of police they ever had in the state of Wyoming. Everyone in this town loves Jim.

people. They come here with the Army or the Air Force. This is why I have to get out and work real hard, because the people that I talked to two years ago are not here anymore.

The Wyoming community that we grew up in, my brothers and I, was a sort of ''we'' community and a ''we'' state. And we're losing that. We used to do everything, like my granddaddy used to say, ''on the shake of a hand.''

My dad wanted all of us to go to school and he wanted us to go to the best school. I thought I would like to go out of the state of Wyoming. At the time they only had forty-eight states, so I had the names of all the states, except Wyoming,

Now I'm A-OK up there in the legislature until I put in a bill for a Martin Luther King holiday. Then the silence comes across. But I get up there and I talk about Martin Luther King and why we should have the holiday and that this is the Equality State.

I've been told many times in the legislature, ''There're not enough blacks here to qualify for a holiday.'' And then I'll say to them, ''The things that he did were for all of us, not just for blacks. Freedom for everybody, not just me.''

So the people ask me, when I run, ''Are you going to go back up there with it?'' I say, ''You can count on this: if I'm there, the legislation will be there.''

When Liz Byrd entered the House of Representatives of Wyoming in 1981, she became the first black legislator elected since statehood in 1890. In 1986, during her third term, she retired from a teaching career that spanned thirty-seven years. In 1988, she was elected to the Wyoming State Senate. In 1990, when the State Legislature of Wyoming finally passed the measures needed to make Martin Luther King, Jr.'s birthday a paid holiday in the state, it was a fine example of her tenacity and determination. Byrd is a life member of the NAACP and a member of the Delta Sigma Theta Sorority. In 1993, she was honored with the Equality Day Award in appreciation for her contributions to the equality of Wyoming women and received the 1993 Wyoming Education Award. Her memorabilia, The Harriett Elizabeth Byrd Collection, is at the American Heritage Center, University of Wyoming.

Shirley Chisholm

Born November 30, 1924, in Brooklyn, New York

Shirley Chisholm is the first black woman to have been elected to the United States Congress. She served the 12th Congressional District of Brooklyn for seven terms from 1968 until 1982. In 1972, she made an unprecedented bid for the presidential nomination of the Democratic Party. She is the founder of the National Political Congress of Black Women. Her autobiography, Unbought and Unbossed, *was published in 1970. Although retired for more than fifteen years, the author of* The Good Fight *(1973) remains the model of independence and integrity. In 1993, she refused President Clinton's offer of nomination to the U.S. Ambassadorship to Jamaica. An educator and day-care administrator prior to her political career, Shirley Chisholm has received eighty-three honorary doctorates, numerous citations, and proclamations honoring her years of public service. She was inducted into Black America's Hall of Fame in 1997.*

When I was about six or seven . . . even then I was beginning to show signs of leadership. Only it wasn't called leadership. At that time it was called a rebellious little girl.

To dare say that I wanted to guide the ship of state, people laughed. Some of my friends even went so far as to believe that maybe Shirley was a bit half-cracked. I've looked to no man walking this earth for approval. I've always looked to my conscience and to God.

Back in the forties at Brooklyn College we used to have local white politicians come to the campus to speak. And I remember towards the end of his speech, this politician said, "Black people will advance someday, but black people are always going to need to have white people leading them." I will never forget that as long as I live.

That did something to me. I became angry. I don't even think I became so angry at the words as much as the way he said it, with scorn and arrogance, with a know-it-all attitude. And in my mind's eye, I said, "I'm going to show you someday there'll be at least one black person who's not going to accept that."

From those days in clubhouse projects on the local level, people began to mobilize. Before they sent me to the New York State Assembly in 1964, I had battles with some black men who wanted a seat. When the people saw how well I did in the Assembly and they wanted to send me to Congress, that's when the real battle began to take place.

Brooklyn, which has such a large minority population, had never had a representative for the minority population in the House. And now that the time was coming, to talk about sending a woman! The regular Democratic machine was very powerful and it was going to select the black it wanted.

There's all kinds of things they did behind the scenes to stop me. But I knew within myself that God would never permit me to continue to rebel, to fight, and to accept all of the misinterpretation, misunderstanding, slander, snide remarks, racist remarks, all kinds of remarks, if He did not know that I could handle it.

All I've heard for the twenty-eight years that I've been an active politician is "political suicide." And here I am.

Service is the rent that you pay for room on this earth.

I had gone into a number of states and said, "The time has come to change America. Someday, somewhere, somehow, someone other than a white male could be President." I moved into the Presidential bid and that was the worst campaign I ever went through in my life in terms of almost being destroyed by men. They never attacked me in terms of my ability and articulation. It was always an attack based on my gender.

I was surprised, particularly because I was a black woman who had proven herself. I expected criticism from the white community in practically everything I would do. But from my own, it hurt.

I have met far more discrimination as a woman than being black in the field of politics. Why should black men be any different from white men, brown men, pink men, whatever? They're all a part of the male gender, who for so many years had preconceived notions and stereotypical thinking about the role of women.

But in spite of it all, I went to the Democratic convention in 1972 and did my thing and began to open the way for women to think that they can run. I ended up with 158 delegate votes. Sixteen years later Jesse Jackson runs and comes up with over a thousand delegates.

One of the things that's always been fascinating to me, as I go across this country speaking before women's groups and on college campuses, is for white people to come up to me and say, "My God! You're one of the most dynamic speakers we've ever heard." And some of them say to me, "You must have been exposed to white people." These are white people who have not been exposed to an educated black woman.

If I didn't have a sense of humor, I would have cracked up a long time ago. But I do. I could laugh at myself, and I could laugh at others. Believe it or not, I'm a great dancer. I've won prizes in dance. I go to a disco every so often. I can get on down. I can.

In the early sixties when I became a part of the National Organization for Women, black and Hispanic women cut me up. They said, "How can you join that organization when it's really had some racist white women in there?" I said, "You cannot fight by being on the outside complaining and whining. You have to get on the inside to be able to assess their strengths and weaknesses and then move in."

Nobody calls on black women to find out what they're thinking about because we're always part of somebody else's agenda. We've been helping everybody except ourselves. The time has come and we will be no longer the complacent, placid, armchair recipients of whatever anybody is going to bequeath to us. I want to organize black women in this country so that they'll become a force to be dealt with.

Wyomia Tyus

Born August 29, 1945, in Griffin, Georgia

I grew up with three older brothers. My father made sure they allowed me to play on the team. I had to be not just good, but extra good because I was a girl. A lot of times that's the first thing the guys would say, "We don't want a girl on our team." My brothers would say, "That's okay, we'll take her." Next time we'd go play, I was the first to be chosen.

A lot of our friends had to stay home and pick cotton. My father would not allow it. We didn't have money, but we never had to work as children. Our responsibility was to go to school and get an education.

Our coach would always say that you could be on top today and down in the gutter tomorrow. So you have to prepare for that tomorrow. That's how I looked at it.

When I traveled, I would try to see as much as I could, because I never knew if I was going to get back. I was a scared little kid. I never had any idea that I would go to Russia or Poland, Germany and Japan, places like that. It made me grow as a human being.

In 1964, I had just started college. Edith McGuire was also on the team and we're both from Georgia. After we came back from Japan we went to Atlanta and they had a big parade for us. And then it was the afternoon, and we had to start our school semester. All that was forgotten.

In going to Europe I always thought they really treated the women a lot different, much better. The women athletes got as much praise as the men, if not more. I'd look at the European women who competed when I did and they didn't win a gold medal and they're still looked upon as real great athletes. They're definitely put in the limelight.

It's not like I was out there running and not knowing what's going on in the country. I knew what was going on, but I felt this is not something that is going to bog me down and not let me participate. The only way I was going to make a difference for myself or any other black person is to say the hurdles were there and do what I had to do.

Just because I went to the Olympics and won medals, that did not change me. I'm still that same human being that you did not want in the door in the first place. Just because I won the medals does not change my color, my thinking, or the way you feel about me.

In 1968, there was a lot going on, unrest as far as blacks were concerned. At Tennessee State we had riots on campus and we were really going through what the sixties were all about.

Most of the time people looked at athletes and said they were not involved. Then Tommy Smith, Lee Evans, John Carlos, and Harry Edwards [the athletes and their adviser] suggested that because of what was happening to blacks in America, we should not go to the Olympic Games in Mexico. They're on the West Coast and we're in Tennessee. We were never consulted about anything. We were women and they weren't concerned. We had not come together as a unit. Individuals would have to do what they felt was right.

Well, Tommy Smith won the 200 meters and John Carlos got third and they went on the victory stand, raised a black-gloved fist, and bowed their head as the national anthem was played. There was so much uproar, basically from Americans, that they kicked them out of the Olympic village.

What John Carlos and Tommy Smith did on their victory stand was something they believed in and wanted to do. It was so dramatic and to the point. It brought more awareness to what was happening to blacks in America.

After that most of the athletes wanted to do something in support. We decided to wear black arm bands, black socks, something dark. I wore dark shorts after winning my gold medal in the relay, I dedicated my medal to them for what they did.

I never really dealt with the women's issue very much because I could never get past the black issue. When you look at it, you have a double minority here. What can I do, being I'm black and I am a woman? Which one of these issues are you going to tackle first?

You are in a game of life, so to speak, because you have your ups and downs. When you're up, everybody's with you. When you're down, you're really by yourself. In sports people are taught when you're down you really fight to get back up. When it comes to a real-life situation, for some reason, we lose all that instinct that we have to fight and keep going, and we give in.

There's been many a time when I've won a race but I didn't feel good about winning it because I didn't do the things that it took to win. I was just able to beat my competition.

Starting all over, it's kind of difficult saying where you want to go. You go step by step, waiting and waiting. And, I guess, being a sprinter, it's hard to wait. I just want to get to the finish line.

Wyomia Tyus was the first athlete to win a gold medal for the 100-meter race in two consecutive Olympics, the 1964 Games in Tokyo and the 1968 Games in Mexico City, where she set a new world record. As part of the United States 4 × 100 relay team, she also won a silver medal in 1964 and the gold in 1968. A member of the U.S. Olympic Hall of Fame and the Women's Sports Hall of Fame, she lives in Los Angeles, where she is a naturalist at an outdoor education camp run by the Los Angeles Unified School District.

Ruby Dee

Born October 27, 1927, in Cleveland, Ohio

Ruby Dee's luminous performances on stage, film, and television have made her one of the most recognized actresses in America. From her first major Broadway role in Anna Lucasta *in 1946, she developed into a versatile performer with extensive stage credits. She has worked with her husband, actor-author Ossie Davis, on numerous projects, notably the 1981 television series* With Ossie and Ruby. *A collection of her poetry,* My One Good Nerve, *was published in 1986. Dee has also adapted two African folktales into books for children:* Two Ways to Count to Ten, *which won the Literary Guild Award in 1989, and* Tower to Heaven, *published in 1991. In 1994, Dee and Davis received the Silver Circle Award from the Academy of Television Arts and Sciences. In 1995, they were given the National Medal of Arts.* With Ruby and Ossie—In This Life Together *is a joint chronicle of their lives and careers, published in 1998—just in time to be part of their 50th anniversary celebration.*

You just try to do everything that comes up. Get up an hour earlier, stay up an hour later, make the time. Then you look back and say, "Well, that was a neat piece of juggling there—school, marriage, babies, career." The enthusiasms took me through the action, not the measuring of it or the reasonableness.

I like the idea of people striving to be better and to make the world better. The world has improved mostly through people who are unorthodox, who do unorthodox things. They're always shaking up the establishment. When we saw such people, we appreciated them and did what we could to support them.

That's what being young is all about. You have the courage and the daring to think that you can make a difference. You're not prone to measure your energies in time. You're not likely to live by equations.

Marriage is a process, we've discovered. The wedding is the event. It takes a long time to be really married. One marries many times at many levels within a marriage. If you have more marriages than you have divorces within the marriage, you're lucky and you stick it out.

We just did what we had to. And to feel the consequences . . . well, they just were. Life for an actor is tough anyway, so how can you tell what's contributing to it? What's contributing to the toughness in our life?

I absolutely love acting, when I'm acting. I absolutely love writing, when I'm writing. I tend to write things that are not serious better than I do things that are serious. That surprised me about myself.

We did a series on PBS [*With Ossie and Ruby*] that was really very satisfying, good work that we were proud of. We worked with a lot of authors that we admired. We traveled on tour, exploring, talking about authors, and introducing people to those who put the "black experience" in perspective and made us look at ourselves outside of the great problem of racism and white folks.

Practically every woman I read I fall in love with. I appreciate women like Alice Walker, Margaret Walker, Toni Morrison, Rosa Guy, Toni Cade Bambara. They put me in context as a person. They did a lot for me. I've always studied literature in school—French, Spanish, and English literature. I wasn't really aware of the astonishing work of black people until I got out of college.

We're doing a mad dance just trying to find out how to exist in this world. Racism just blinds us to the real problems that face us all. It's easier and more dramatic to say, "Oh, white folks are terrible and men are dogs and there's a lot of unfairness." And I say, "So this is life." But I get angry, too.

Racism, feelings of superiority, it's a sickness. I truly believe that racism is taking second place to classism. Classism and greed are making insignificant all other kinds of isms.

I see great progress in the growth of white America. I like to look at that part of it. I like to see that we're growing closer together as people. I think maybe there's growth in the undertow.

I don't call myself an optimist. I dare not judge the world because the fools have written it this way or drawn it or treated it so, or that people come on the scene and think that the world begins and ends at this time with me and with them.

Leontine T. C. Kelly

Born March 5, 1920, in Washington, D.C.

Bishop Kelly is first black woman bishop of a major religious denomination in the United States. In 1984, she was elected head of the United Methodist Church in the San Francisco area, comprising nearly 400 churches and 100,000 members. Following her retirement in 1988, she became a visiting professor at the Pacific School of Religion in Berkeley.

My father was a Methodist minister. I was born in the parsonage of Mount Zion Methodist Episcopal Church in the Georgetown section of Washington, D.C. One of the stories in our family is that the second black bishop elected in the Methodist church baptized me when I was three months old. The story goes that when he handed me back to my mother, he said, ''How I wish you were a boy, so that my mantle could fall on you.'' He'd probably turn over in his grave at the idea of a woman being a bishop in the church.

All four of my father's daughters said that we would never marry a minister. So, certainly, there was no thought of *being* one. I was a schoolteacher and that, I felt, was my ministry. I did not enter the ministry until my husband, a minister, died in 1969. I had been a certified lay speaker in the church for twelve years.

It's difficult for me not to preach. My children would tell you that, even as a mama. When the district superintendent asked my youngest son what he thought about me going in the ministry, he said, ''She's been preaching all my life.''

There has been an ordination and an acceptance, but women still work toward equality in the church. It isn't there yet, it's like society.

Some people use the Corinthian scripture of Paul saying women should not speak in the church. But we could find our own scriptures to substantiate why women should be allowed to speak.

I believe in a called ministry, a sense of assurance that there is something specific for you to do. For me, it was a year after my husband's death, the people asked me to serve the church that he pastored [in Edwardsville, Virginia]. Paul didn't call me. I believe God called me to the ordained ministry. I was willing to go that journey and it has been sustained.

Many people say you can prove whatever you want to from the Bible. But as a black person, what I look for in the Bible is a sense of my own freedom and acceptance by God and the sense of liberation that is there for me. And that word comes through very clearly.

As a child I asked my father, how could black people be Christian? How could they accept it, when the very persons that enslaved them taught them Christianity? My father said that in God there was the strength and the source for patience to wait for freedom. That was his sense of it. What I have found, of course, is that everybody wasn't waiting. People were working.

As children in Cincinnati, we located a station of the underground railway in the basement of our house. It went from the house to the church. When my father told us about it, he said that the witness of this church was not the wood brought all the way from Italy for the great beams. The real witness of that church was in the cellar. Someone had taken the risk to move against society and the government. It was a sanctuary movement of those days. I was excited about what kind of preaching was going on in a church like that.

My father not only preached, but he also ran a church that was the economic, cultural, and political center of the community. He also became an Ohio legislator.

We were not reared that politics was not a part of a Christian's duty. If we were going to pray for liberation and equality, then we also had to work for it.

Another question was, Why do we stay in a major denomination that by its own policies does not accept us? Our whole concept was that we were in mission to the church. Where the church saw us as objects of mission, we saw the major church as a mission field for us, knowing that if you ever got the major churches of this country straight, then you were working on the country at the same time.

I was about eight years old and I opened the door one day and there was Mary McLeod Bethune. I remember sitting on the floor playing as my mother and she talked. Mrs. Bethune was saying that colored women need to stop playing bridge and start building bridges.

I've never been accused of not being outspoken. I crusaded for women as well as all ethnics in the church. Our proclamations and resolutions are great. We have yet to live them out.

As a country we have really been lulled into some kind of sense of superiority, as if we deserve some special reward from God. Our American children are about to be the only unilingual children in the world. And we pass legislation as if English were the king's language, I mean, God's language.

We privatize our religion such that it makes it safe for people to be Christian. And Christianity is not safe. If you're going to follow Jesus, then it's risky to do that.

For me, the crux of the gospel message is the way we share power. One of the things women bring to the situation in terms of sharing power is new styles of leadership. I am no less the bishop. I know where the buck stops and who is responsible. But that doesn't mean that I have to exert power in such a way that other people feel they are less than who they are because of who I am.

Margaret Walker Alexander

Born July 7, 1915, in Birmingham, Alabama
Died November 30, 1998, in Chicago, Illinois

My mother read poetry to me before I could read, and I can't remember when I couldn't read. We grew up with books. I don't think you can write if you don't read. You can't read if you can't think. Thinking, reading, and writing all go together. When I was about eight, I decided that the most wonderful thing, next to a human being, was a book.

I finished grade school when I was eleven and a half. I finished high school when I was fourteen. I went to college when I was fifteen. I would have finished at eighteen but I had to stay out a year. My father said I was precocious.

He told me the first three lessons I learned about poetry: you must have pictures, you must have music, and you must have meaning. And I learned that prose has to have rhythm, pictures, and meaning, too.

I was twenty-two when I wrote "For My People." With the exception of the last stanza, I wrote it in fifteen minutes on a typewriter. That was one of those things that came out whole. That's been more than fifty years ago and I haven't changed in my idea. I've read that poem all over the country.

I wouldn't have a need to write without the problems that I face as a black woman in America. The three enemies of black women are racism, sexism, and fascism. I've been fighting them all my life.

I taught nearly forty years and I taught my students that every person is a human being. Every human personality is sacred, potentially divine. Nobody is any more than that and nobody can be any less.

A man came in my kitchen where I had a thing that was supposed to be a washer-dryer that never worked. I said it had to go. He was determined to fix it. He said I must have done so-and-so to it. When I said no, he said, "Don't you dispute my word." I said, "Why?" "'Cause I'm a white man." I told him to get out of my house and don't ever come back.

Do you see what's happened to his brain? He thinks he's something 'cause he's white. His skin makes him somebody. And do you know that is the trouble with the country today?

Segregation is over legally, but what it has done to the mind of both black and white is not over.

The black church and the white church are very different churches. If you listen on Sunday morning to the television preachers, or you go into any white church, the preacher is talking about personal salvation. Are you saved? Where will you spend eternity? Are you living right? And that kind of thing. He never talks about a social gospel. He doesn't talk about the brotherhood of man, that all men are your brothers, that God is the Father of us all. That's the black church. The black church says, "You know all of us are Your children." They're both preaching the gospel as they understand it, but one's a social gospel and one's a personal gospel. I think my father preached both.

My father, a Methodist minister and a highly trained theologian of the modern school, taught us to respect all religions. He could read Hebrew, Latin, and Greek. He spoke five languages including Hindustani. He knew Castilian Spanish. He was as fine a scholar as I have met anywhere.

You can't do but three things with money, my father taught me. You can spend it, save it, or give it away. With every dollar you save a dime, you spend a quarter or fifty cents, and you give some of it away. To me, that's a spiritual use of money.

Everything I'm looking at, I'm going to leave. There are no pockets in coffins.

My mentors have all been men. Langston Hughes was the first real live poet I ever saw. I admired him very much and spent a great deal of time with him, off and on, through thirty-five years. The second great person was W.E.B. Du Bois. He was the greatest of our thinkers in this century. And the third person who influenced me more in terms of social, political, and economic thinking than anybody else was Richard Wright.

For the first time in ten years I was able to give a coherent, unimpassioned speech about *Roots* and Alex Haley. After my lawsuit, most of the newspapers showed me as this agitated, bitter, angry old woman. Nobody was concerned about my charges of plagiarism, they laughed it off. That was the biggest rip-off of my life.

I think black women, whether they were strong women or whether they were beaten and broken down, had a belief in the goodness of the future. They always wanted another world that would be better for their children than it had been for them. The black woman has deep wells of spiritual strength. She doesn't know how she's going to feed her family in the morning, but she prays and in the morning, out of thin air, she makes breakfast.

Margaret Walker Alexander published her first book of poetry, For My People, *in 1942 and the historical novel* Jubilee *in 1966. She earned her master's and doctoral degrees from the University of Iowa for these creative classics. Her poem, "For My People," has become one of the literary anthems of the black community. After four decades of teaching, she retired as Emeritus Professor of English at Jackson State University in Jackson, Mississippi. Her biography of the novelist,* Richard Wright: Daemonic Genius, *was published in 1988. Her most recent book of poetry,* This Is My Century: New and Collected Poems, *was published in 1989, and an audio recording,* Margaret Walker Interviews with Kay Bonetti, *was released by the American Audio Prose Library in 1991.*

Rachel Robinson

Born July 19, 1922, in Los Angeles, California

Rachel Robinson is the chairperson of the Jackie Robinson Foundation, which she formed in honor of her late husband, the first black man to integrate major-league baseball. As a professional in psychiatric nursing, she has held clinical, teaching, and administrative positions in New York and Connecticut. She is president of the J. R. Development Corporation, which built six housing developments in fifteen years. Mrs. Robinson is the recipient of nine honorary doctoral degrees, and numerous awards. Among the more recent are Turner Broadcasting's Trumpet Award (1992), the Branch Rickey Award (1995), the National Urban League's Humanitarian Award (1996), the Arthur Ashe Award, and the Eleanor Roosevelt Val-Kill Medal (both in 1998). Her book, Jackie Robinson, An Intimate Portrait, *was published in 1996.*

My father was gassed in France during the last days of World War I. Because of that he developed a severe cardiac condition. He was a very active, wonderful guy, but he had to retire in his forties. And I, as the middle child and a female child, was taught to be a very active partner in the family.

Both my father and Jack had a strong and positive sense of identification with our race: no ambivalence, no doubts, and a clarity about who they were. But my belief in myself and identification with my people needed strengthening. I got a large measure of that from Jack, from the very first day I saw him on the UCLA campus. Here was this ebony colored man wearing white shirts all the time. I thought he must be proud to come out that way. Instead of playing down the intensity of color, he displayed it with great confidence.

The bonding between us, the way we sort of grew together and grew up together made our relationship more than a marriage. We were what I like to call a working pair. We were essential to each other. He succeeded in part because we succeeded.

It is very easy to be drawn into being a professional widow. People want to preserve the widow of a great man in that role and I saw it as a trap—one that I recognized long before Jack died, because it was also a potential trap to be just Mrs. Jackie Robinson. It was important, but I had to work at becoming Rachel Robinson, too.

Shortly after Jack retired from baseball, I returned to school for a graduate degree and became a psychiatric nurse. I wanted to become a professional person with all of its rewards and challenges. Years later, when I decided to take over the construction company that Jack was just starting when he died, my experiences as a nurse, teacher and administrator helped me carry on without him.

In 1973, I founded the Jackie Robinson Foundation, and that has been a very important part of my work. We support minority education and leadership development. We have given full, four-year scholarships, and a wealth of supportive services to hundreds of students around the country. We call them the Jackie Robinson Scholars.

The individual can make a difference. Many people say "Well, there's no movement to join," and "How are we going to create change without an organized movement?" If Jack symbolizes anything, it is that the committed individual can find a way of making a difference.

Jack entitled his autobiography *I Never Had It Made*, and in the book he said that he couldn't rejoice in his good fortune while his brothers were, as he put it, "down in a deep hole hollering for help and not being heard." It really is about having succeeded to a certain degree but feeling that until the masses of people are living decently, none of us have secured our place in America.

When the Carnegie Foundation says that the black male is an "endangered species," to some people that's just a headline, but to me that is a threat that cannot go unanswered. There is a man—a black man—who leans against my office building on 14th Street and I have developed the habit of stopping and talking with him. I feel he's a part of me, even though I'm on the penthouse floor and he's down there existing in the most degrading circumstances. That's a part of me down there, and anything I do for him or others I'm doing for myself.

These feelings are captured in the Makonde sculpture that my son David imports from his home in Tanzania. They are carved interlocking figures that support each other to form a pyramid called the "Tree of Life." The sculptures symbolize the concepts of sharing and strength through unity, from generation to generation: we balance on each others' shoulders and even if you stand on my head it's okay, if it will hold you up.

I have taken all of my children to Africa and now I've started taking grandchildren. But it's not a trend or a fad for us. It's an aspect of personality development that is firm and fixed and essential. David and my daughter Sharon feel, and I agree, that until we as Afro-Americans are fully rejoined with Africa, in terms of pride and knowledge of our ancestry, we will never be whole people.

I believe that we, as a people, need a stronger more unified approach to social change, but I know we will always have to work with diverse attitudes and postures. There will be a range from those who do nothing to those who devote their lives to the problems facing us.

I feel so proud of the southern blacks who stayed in the south during the forties and fifties and sixties and said, "I'm not moving. This is my town." I'm proud of them because now we have something to go back to because they stood and fought. We have something to build on. That's progress.

If I have one motto for myself, it's "Fight Back." I almost pin it on the walls around my house. We're engaged in a struggle that will be on-going for generations, I fear. So the willingness to fight back and the psychological stamina and discipline to keep focused on basic goals is essential.

Gloria Dean Randle Scott

Born April 14, 1938, in Houston, Texas

Dr. Gloria Scott is the president of Bennett College, founded in 1873 in Greensboro, North Carolina. Before assuming that office in 1987, she held several faculty and administrative positions at black colleges, including the vice-presidency of Clark College in Atlanta. She received three degrees, including a Ph.D. in higher education, from the University of Indiana at Bloomington. She was elected national president of the Girl Scouts in 1975—the first black woman to serve in that position—and held office for three years. Among her many contributions to Bennett College has been the creation of the Women's Leadership Institute. She is also founder of Africa University in Mutare, Zimbabwe. Dr. Scott has been proclaimed a Woman of Distinction by the states of Texas and North Carolina, and the Delta Sigma Theta sorority.

The one thing that really used to bother me as a little girl was why I couldn't go to the library. The public libraries in Houston became open to black people either during my senior year in high school or after I had graduated. When it was first opened, I walked through every inch of the library. That was my sort of defiance.

When I was in the second or third grade I had a paper route. It was the *Houston Informer*, the black newspaper. There was this little store that had a group of men in it all the time—one was blind. The first time I went to sell papers there this man said, "I can't buy a paper. I can't read." So I said, "Well, I could read it to you." And that's how we started our relationship. He'd buy a newspaper, I'd read it to him, and then I could take it and resell it.

When you say "the civil rights movement," I say "the *modern* civil rights movement." If you know your history, you know there were many riots, early, where black people just rose up against the treatment being given them. In East Texas, where my family is from—in fact, in many places in Texas—there was the notion that there would have to be change, but it was going to have to be actively brought about.

We heard from our great uncles who had gone to World War One how a lot of foreign people treated black people much better than they could be treated in our own country.

Every black person who had some measure of achievement and visibility was my hero. Like Joe Louis. Everybody didn't have a radio, so people would gather around on various porches to listen to all of his fights. Little children and adults would do better than commentators at calling the fight and they couldn't even see it. But there was no reason for white people to treat us like this and Joe Louis proved it.

There was a white man who owned property, little two-bedroom shotgun houses, and that's how he made his millions, off of black people. There was a black woman who worked for him as his bookkeeper who persuaded him to leave his money in trust for black high school kids. He had no family, only a dog, and he left some money for the dog. Beyond that, the money stayed in trust for black kids to go to college. I think I was the second to receive one of the E. E. Worthing scholarships. They were a thousand dollars a year. In 1955 that was a lot of money. That's what I went to college on.

After I got a master's [in zoology], I worked for a research institute on the interdisciplinary team and I did the genetics lab in embryology. Then I started teaching biology in Indianapolis in 1961, and it turned out I was going to be the first black teacher at this predominantly white college.

In the process of doing that I decided that what I really wanted to do was work in black colleges for black kids. My husband and I have always team-taught, and we decided that what we could give was our knowledge and our experience, and *that* could be shared, duplicated, and extended by working in a black college setting. I knew there were hundreds of thousands of black kids just like me, poor, who didn't have access to a number of things, who needed to have people to help move them along.

To get through, you have to have a base. I see on whose shoulders we stand. Some of us only got through because *they* didn't. And that's a critical responsibility for the generation you're in, to help provide the shoulders, the direction, and the support for those generations who come behind.

About 1965, the Girl Scouts did some major studies looking at why so few minority girls and adults were involved. They went through a review and came out with the notion that there was a lot of institutional racism. Even where there were good intent and good programs, there were barriers. There were no adults like me for girls to see in scouting. So we really moved off in a whole different direction from about 10 percent [minority girls] in the mid-sixties to 25 or 30 percent now.

Part of the manifestation of racism is that we don't value diversity. We've got to have a superior something or a great chain of inferiority, instead of looking at the fact that each is different and diverse and to value the whole of that. Probably never will we really be where we want to be until we can strengthen the value of diversity—not to have a hierarchy, but to accept.

I see Bennett strengthening its historical past and its present in such a way that it's responsive to not only careers but also personal development. One of the things we are working on is the development of a comprehensive research basis to provide a kind of chronicle of what black women have really done in America. I hope to see Bennett forge linkages with women in Africa and Third World nations.

I hope that we reclaim the highly critical area of producing good teachers. I don't think that it has to be important just for black kids. I think white children ought to have healthy exposure to black people in leadership and adult roles, too.

You can focus on the obstacles, or you can go on and decide what you do about it. To me, it breaks down to that: you can do and not just be.

Marian Wright Edelman

Born June 6, 1939, in Bennettsville, South Carolina

Service was as much a part of my upbringing as eating breakfast and going to school. It isn't something that you do in your spare time. It was clear that it was the very purpose of life. In that context, you're not obligated to win. You're obligated to keep trying, to keep doing the best you can every day.

Helping others had the highest value. There was no black home for the aged in South Carolina when I was growing up, so my daddy, who was a minister, started one across the street, and we all had to get out there and cook and serve. My mother died a few years ago, still running that home for the aged. She was cooking for six old people, all of them younger than she was.

The outside world told black kids when I was growing up that we weren't worth anything. It told us we were second-class, that poor kids weren't valued. But our parents said it wasn't so and our churches and our schoolteachers said it wasn't so. They believed in us and we, therefore, believed in ourselves.

I never had a chance not to do what I do. Law school was a tool. I didn't have any interest or aptitude in the law, but it was what was needed then. When I moved down to Mississippi, there were 900,000 blacks and three black lawyers, two of whom had never gone to law school.

People would do their voter registration and they would be thrown off their plantations the next day. In 1964 and 1965 courageous ordinary people gave up their little homes and their food, withstood bombings and shootings, and lost everything to exercise the right to vote that young people don't utilize today. It runs me wild.

Ordinary women of grace are, in a sense, my real role models. What always struck me is how unbitter they were. They had the capacity to keep struggling. I think that is a message that this quick-fix culture needs, this culture that thinks things should be solved instantly or cheaply. They're always searching for cheap grace.

Poor black folks, who began to go to school and learn how to read and write with their three-, four-, and five-year-olds in the Head Start center, didn't have anybody in Washington to watch out for their interests. Somebody would say, "Cut off their money." And it became clear to me that the poor needed somebody. General Motors hires lots of paid lobbyists to take care of their interests. The poor didn't have anybody to do that, children didn't have anybody to do that.

The issue for me when I moved to Washington in 1968 was how could one provide a countervoice to the powerful in order to see poor people have a chance to help themselves and their children.

In our society we have made a distinction between our kids and other folks' children because of the history of race and class. Because of racial discrimination, and because we tend to judge the poor, we have been willing to punish the children for their parents.

The work force of the year 2000 is our preschoolers today. One in four of them is poor. For black kids, one in two is poor. One in six hasn't got any health insurance. One in two has got a mother in the labor force and is not getting decent child care. One in five is going to be a teen parent. One in seven is going to drop out of school. This is a recipe for national catastrophe.

We lose about ten thousand children every year to poverty. That's more kids over a five-year period than we lost in the Vietnam war. But where is the outrage?

If the foundation of your national house is crumbling, you don't say you can't afford to fix it and continue to build multitrillion dollar defense fences around to protect it from something without. It's crazy.

We may well be the first generation of adults whose children not only don't do as well as we do, but may be worse when we get done. We may be in the midst of the first downwardly mobile American generation.

We are making a big effort to see if the Children's Defense Fund can't do massive public education. Our goal is to show the nation that preventive investment in kids has got to become the cornerstone of the American domestic policy.

If you're serious about an educated work force and you're serious about giving kids that early foundation, then you can't throw them out there into cheap baby-sitting. We've got to invest in it and that's going to cost a little money. And the issue is not whether we're going to spend the money, it's when and how much. Because you'll pay for them in prison or you'll pay for them in day care.

Children cannot eat rhetoric and they cannot be sheltered by commissions. I don't want to see another commission that studies the needs of kids. We need to help them.

I am an outsider. I am not a linear person. I couldn't work within a government structure. What I want to do is see that this country feeds hungry kids. The legacy I want to leave is a child-care system that says that no kid is going to be left alone or left unsafe.

In 1965, Marian Wright Edelman became the first black woman admitted to the bar in Mississippi. A graduate of Spelman College and Yale Law School, she directed the NAACP Legal Defense and Education Fund in Mississippi and New York from 1964 to 1968. She is the founder, president, and highly effective spokesperson of the Children's Defense Fund. Since 1973, this advocacy group has lobbied in support of health, welfare, and justice for children and their families. Mrs. Edelman is the author of Families in Peril: An Agenda for Social Change, The Measure of Our Success: A Letter to My Children and Yours, and Guide My Feet: Meditations and Prayers on Loving and Working For Children. She is the recipient of many honorary degrees and awards; the Albert Schweitzer Humanitarian Prize and the Heinz Award are but two that have heralded her efforts. She was awarded the prestigious MacArthur Fellowship in 1985.

Elizabeth Catlett

Born April 15, 1919, in Washington, D.C.

Elizabeth Catlett is a distinguished sculptor and lithographer. Among her major commissions are a life-size bronze bust of poet Phillis Wheatley for Jackson State University, a ten-foot bronze of musician Louis Armstrong for the city of New Orleans, and a twenty-four-foot bronze relief for Howard University. A resident of Mexico since 1946 and a Mexican citizen since 1962, she was the first woman professor of sculpture in the School of Fine Arts of the National Autonomous University of Mexico. In 1998, a fifty-year retrospective, Elizabeth Catlett Sculpture, *premiered at the Neuberger Museum of Art at Purchase College, State University of New York, with tour stops in Houston, Baltimore, Atlanta, and Mexico City during 1998 and 1999. Her work is in the collections of major museums across the country and around the world. Her most recent public commission was a seven-foot stone figure of Sojourner Truth for the Sacramento City Gardens.*

When I first started at Howard University, I was very frivolous and social-minded. I was in design. I was going to be a commercial artist and make a lot of money. I learned from James Porter [of the Howard art faculty] the seriousness of being an artist. He taught me that you have to discipline yourself.

Then when I went to the University of Iowa, Grant Wood [painter of *American Gothic*] taught me that you should work with what you know the most about. That's what he did. He painted Iowa, which is what he knew the most about.

I was working always with the black theme. I did a whole series on black women. Nobody was doing black women. I am a black woman. That's what I know the most about.

The chairman of the art department at Iowa asked what degree I wanted to apply for. I said, "I want a Master of Fine Arts." He said, "Nobody has ever gotten a Master of Fine Arts, and you can't be the first one. So I would suggest you apply for the Master of Arts." And I said, "Why can't I be the first one?" He said, "Because you're a woman," and he didn't add the other part, but I could see he was thinking it.

After the oral examination, they asked me to wait outside. I could hear voices raised. Finally they opened the door and congratulated me because I was going to get the Master of Fine Arts degree. The other students were very happy for me and they said, "Now you've opened it up."

Dr. William Du Bois once told me, "Never take a step backward or you never stop running." I never forgot it.

I studied with a very famous French sculptor who was a refugee in New York. I learned to experiment from him. I used to discuss things with him. He would say, "Why do you want to do a black mother and child? That's national, you should do international art, then everybody could relate to it. I do international figures." And I would say, "So, you do a musician or a poet and everybody relates. But I notice you did a French poet and he has his poem written in French."

When I first came to New York I lived in a fancy building on Sugar Hill in Harlem. I got right into the middle of a lot of cultural things. Aaron Douglas, the painter, lived downstairs. Langston Hughes would come in. I met Paul Robeson.

I was invited to work at the George Washington Carver School, which was a people's school in Harlem. This is all during World War II. The students paid three dollars per course. We had courses like "Meet the Author" and "What Do You Know About Economics?" We had sculpture, which I taught. All the teachers were voluntary teachers. Our students were working people, like domestic workers, people that were hungry for some kind of education and culture. We had people from the West Indies, Czechoslovakia, China, Greece, and Italy. It was a tremendous experience for me.

I always did sew and I taught how to make a dress. I'd say, "First, make it an art color. See whether we look nice in red and turquoise blue and all kinds of colors."

I used to write proposals for Rosenwald grants for people and they would get them, so I wrote one for me. And I got the grant. Ever since I saw Diego Rivera's murals, I wanted to go to Mexico. The Rosenwald wasn't that much money and Mexico was cheap. So I went to Mexico to work on a series of paintings, prints, and sculptures to exhibit throughout the South. I wanted black people to see art. My art is to serve black people. That's one of my main aims.

I went to work at the Taller de Gráfica Popular, a graphic arts workshop. What interested me in the Taller was that they had a declaration of purpose. They worked collectively. I was working with very political people in Mexico.

I think white middle-class feminists are involved with white middle-class women, and not with *women*, or they would see what plight black women and Asian women and Chicano women are in. This is the difference between the movement in the United States and the movement in Mexico. We work with women that don't have shoes. I don't think it's a special strength in black women. Most women that have to fight for survival get a special strength sooner or later.

In Mexico I can work at being an artist, which I couldn't do in the States. When I taught, I couldn't function as an artist much. In Mexico, we can pay our income tax with art.

It's not the good artists or even the great artists who are bought and sold, it's who makes the money for the people that are buying and selling.

When you find someone who is very talented, very sensitive, and who works very hard, then you have a good artist.

There is a group of women artists, the Guerrilla Girls, who made a beginning survey on museum exhibitions. Black women were a big zero. No black woman has ever had a show in the Whitney Museum. No black woman has ever had a one-woman show in the Metropolitan Museum. This is where you're going to have to struggle and get recognized.

Jackie Torrence

Born February 12, 1944, in Chicago, Illinois

Sometimes when I'm in a store shopping, I'll feel a certain material or a texture. Something I feel or touch or smell will trigger a story that's been hidden way down deep in my brain, set back in that four-year-old time when I would get up on my grandmother's lap and she would cover me with her apron and we would rock and she would just talk about things.

For the first fourteen years of my life I was ashamed because I was fat, I had two sets of teeth in the roof of my mouth and I couldn't speak, and my classmates snickered at me.

My ninth-grade teacher, Mrs. Abna Lancaster, one of the most incredible people I have ever met, says that in me she found an eagle among her chickens. She worked with me day and night and Saturdays to change my speech. She will tell you that she never taught school, she taught students. We were far beyond everybody else when it was time to become black and beautiful.

I used to push the whites' water fountain when nobody was in the hall. I wanted to see if the water came out white.

Without being certified, I was quite a reference librarian. One day in 1972 it snowed, and nobody could make it to work. I walked and when I got there my boss told me to read the children a story or show them a film or something. I told them a story and they loved it and asked me to tell it again, and I did. And that's how storytelling found Jackie Torrence. I went to town then. I started devouring stories, the Jack tales, the Grandfather tales, every kind of story I could think of.

One Saturday, after a year of storytelling, my daughter Lori and I went out to my best friend's house. It was rainy outside and she was baking bread and the smell filled the cabin and triggered Uncle Remus and my grandmother's stories. Here I'm telling all of these stories from around the world, telling African stories even, and for some reason I had never thought about those stories before then.

I had been hired to perform in the city schools in Atlanta. They got angry with me because I wanted to tell an Uncle Remus story. The principal said, "I wish you would not. We are trying to teach these children pride." And I said, "But, honey, you don't have any pride unless you know where you came from."

I am proud to know that my ancestry was from Africa. I'm proud that my great-grandparents were slaves and they made it through. They must have been strong, because I'm here.

I have found in storytelling a release. I become that story. I become that character. I completely forget about me. You have to be in that story in order to get somebody to see it.

Radio put technology into storytelling and made it sick. TV killed it. Then you were locked into somebody else's sighting of that story. You no longer had the benefit of making that picture for yourself, using your imagination. Storytelling brings back that humanness that we have lost with TV.

You talk to children and they don't hear you. They are television addicts. Mamas bring them home from the hospital and drag them up in front of the set and the great stare-out begins.

It's wonderful when I walk out of school and a child says to me, "I sure did like your movie." I've heard teachers trying to explain that they didn't see a movie. And I thought. "Ha, ha, you're wrong lady. They saw a movie."

Remember, we are working with the Now Generation, the TV Generation, the children who know how to spell relief. That's how much they know. In one story I tell about an old woman who picked up a box, opened it, and said, "What is this white powder?" A little boy in the second grade said, "Aw, it was cocaine." Second grade.

Everywhere I go, there is a full house. People have rediscovered storytelling. You should see the storytelling festivals. Fifteen years of facing audiences, I learned by trial and error. It hasn't been easy, but it's fun.

If it had not been for storytelling, the black family would not have survived. It was the responsibility of the Uncle Remus types to transfer philosophies, attitudes, values, and advice, by way of storytelling using creatures in the woods as symbols.

I wish you could see all my uncles and aunts when we get together and the stories come out. They are storytellers on a higher level than I will ever be.

I'm not fighting any causes. I'm black, everybody can see that, but I am a storyteller for the masses.

Gone are the days when the court storyteller had the king and maybe fifty people in his court. You have to tell stories to fifty thousand people. You have to find big stories, and you have to have enough energy and stamina to do it.

Jackie Torrence is one of American's foremost storytellers. With a repertoire of more than 300 stories from around the world, she specializes in ghost stories, African-American tales, and Appalachian Mountain lore. She has recorded nine albums and performed on radio and television, and in festivals from England to Hawaii. She has also created a new folk work, "Bluestory," in which she combines stories with music, offering audiences a glimpse into the origins of the blues and blues literature. Her latest book, Jackie's Tales, was published in 1998.

Autherine Lucy

Born October 5, 1929, in Shiloh, Alabama

Author Lucy Foster was the first black student to attend the University of Alabama in Tuscaloosa. A 1952 graduate of Miles College in Birmingham, she wanted to further her education. After several years of court battles to gain admission, she was allowed to go to classes for only a few days in February 1956, before riots erupted on campus and she was expelled. In 1988, the university revoked its resolution of expulsion and invited her to enroll again. In 1998, Lucy-Foster retired from teaching in the Alabama Public School system.

We believed in accepting our conditions as they were until the time to move forward. I was thinking, "Now is the time." The reason why I felt that this could be done was because of an article that had been run in the *Birmingham News*. A questionnaire had been given to the students at the University of Alabama, and even though all of them were not in accord that a Negro would attend that university, there were quite a few who said that they would accept it.

I enrolled on the 1st [of February 1956]. I went to class on the 3rd. It seemed as if it was going to be somewhat normal. Every now and then, some of the students would pass by and say, "I hope your stay here will be happy." Some few, not a whole lot.

My parents didn't have much to say. Some of the whites in the community went over to my father's house in Marengo County and told him that if he didn't get me from up there, they were going to kill them and burn the house down. He was concerned, but he didn't tell me not to go.

The morning of February 6th, everything was quiet. I did not know about everything that had happened on the campus overnight. When we got to the building where I took my first class, there were a whole lot of people around and gangs of police cars. When I went in, I just passed through the crowd, said, "Excuse me," walked on in the door and went on up to the classroom.

After we had been in class about ten or fifteen minutes, the Dean of Women appeared in the door and she kept her eyes right on me. She stood there until the class was over and then she said, "Autherine, I'm afraid we're going to have to take you to your next class in the car. That mob out there is waiting for you."

Just as we got in the car, something hit the windshield that shattered it. It didn't hurt us, but I was pretty scared then. They didn't drive up to the building, they put me out at the edge and told me, "Run for the building." I ran and just as I got in that doorway, something hit me on the shoulder. I kept going. As I ran up the steps, they were behind me saying, "Let's kill her, let's kill her." I went in and a lady was there waiting. She turned the lock on the door as soon as I got in. I was just a bundle of nerves. After I got a little bit settled. I saw that it was a rotten egg I had been hit with.

They chanted all day, "Hey, hey, ho, where did Autherine go? Hey, hey, ho, where in the hell did the nigger go?" They just chanted that all day long.

There were times when I was afraid even to the point that I might not get out alive. I feared on February 6th that I might not leave that campus alive. But I would still go forward with it and I prayed for the strength to do that.

I don't hate white people. I hate the idea that someone, black or white, condescends or looks down on me, on anyone. I do get angry about some things, but I went into this with my eyes wide open.

I might get angry, but I can't afford to stay angry. I can't be angry for thinking about how blessed I was. The only thing that hit me from the whole incident was that egg, and it didn't hurt.

I remember thinking this, "I would like to go back. But the truth of the matter is, what kind of studying can I do in a setup like that? If it does not change, I won't be able to really learn anything. Now what am I going to do?"

I received a telegram which said that I was secluded for the safety of the other students on the campus. But if that had been the case, why didn't they close down school? I was a student, too. Why not make it safe for me as well as others?

They didn't intend to let me come back. They were just waiting for something to use to expel me. I said that the university conspired with the mob when they let the mob overrule them. That's what I was expelled for, making those statements.

Recently the university wrote me a letter that said I'm no longer an expelled student. I can now enroll at the university and study there. It's very late. Thirty-two years.

I used to sometimes look back on the situation and see it as somewhat of a failure in my life. Now I look at it from a different perspective. I view it as a stepping-stone in the civil rights movement. A lot of people saw that young woman who seemed so quiet and easygoing, and thought, If she can step out and do a thing like that, then I can too.

The University of Alabama is my alma mater. I just stayed there for three days, but it is still my alma mater. I did not feel evil toward them because I didn't think they were fighting me. They were fighting tradition and change. It just wasn't my time.

Alexa Canady

Born November 7, 1950, in Lansing, Michigan

Dr. Alexa Canady became, at age thirty, the first black woman neurosurgeon in the United States. She completed her medical studies at the University of Michigan with a specialty in pediatric neurosurgery. Certified by the American Board of Neurological Surgery in 1984, she is a professor at Wayne State University in Detroit, where she has been Vice Chairman in the department of Neurosurgery since 1991. Dr. Canady entered the Michigan Women's Hall of Fame in 1989; she is the 1993 recipient of the President's Award of the American Medical Women's Association. In 1995, she was cited as an "Honored Citizen" for her efforts to improve the quality of life in metropolitan Detroit, during activities surrounding the "Living the Dream" exhibition The History of African American Physicians.

My brother and I were the only black students in the local elementary school. During the second grade I did so well on the California reading test that the teacher thought it was inappropriate for me to have done that well. She lied about what scores were mine and, ultimately, she was fired.

Our family lived in the country outside the city of Lansing. We lived there because the man who had owned the property wanted to build a gas station on the corner and the county refused to rezone it. So he said, "I'll fix it," and he sold it to my father.

As a child, I knew a lot of people who didn't have white-collar jobs but who had white-collar educations. That's something you're always aware of, underutilization of education.

Racism was always presented to me as *their* problem and not *our* problem. It affected your behavior, though. What you used to see in the South was excessively formal public behavior. You were always onstage, and aware that you were onstage; somehow this was a different world out there that needed to be treated carefully and thoughtfully .

The civil rights movement made many things possible which would not otherwise have been possible.

People who came out of school with me in the seventies had the feeling that now we're educated and it's different. There were always people who were well educated and it wasn't different. It really had to do with politics and not with education. Education was essential but not a sufficient quality to make your life better.

When I got a residency in neurosurgery, I got it not because I'm smarter than somebody forty years ago, but because the politics were such that they needed a black woman and I was there and qualified.

I had impeccable credentials coming out of medical school, but there was an undercurrent of, "How can you, a black woman, have the audacity to want to do this? Don't you know that you've got a double whammy?" Well, I came along at a time when it offered them a double positive. They could fulfill the quotas and say, "I finished women, I finished blacks, and all it took was one person instead of two." So that became a positive for me.

I think the decision about what you do for a living is not an intellectual one. It's really a visceral decision. Some places you feel at home, and I felt at home in neurosurgery. I couldn't play it nice and safe because that wasn't me.

My husband laughs. I can't watch people get shot and cut up in the movies. It freaks me out. You're being a voyeur, you can't intervene, you can't help. This is a very different quality than going to the emergency room where somebody's got blood and gore all over the place and you can do something.

One of the things I think surgeons have to do is shift emphasis. My job is really not to cut. My job is to help people, which often includes cutting, and that's a very different focus.

You get to be a part of people's families in a very intimate way. You get to see the strengths of the human spirit that can survive terrible, devastating things, perhaps a situation where their child is dying. You can't make it not painful, but you can certainly make it much easier in terms of their understanding of what's happening.

There have been black physicians for a long time, but they had black practices almost exclusively. You'd have black patients who were really sick go to a white doctor, who must be better. But you never had the really sick white patients coming to the black doctor, who must be better. That's really beginning to break down now. I'm the only black neurosurgeon in the city of Detroit.

The other side of racism is that if you get to be where I am and you're black, they figure you must be really damn good and you get a little bonus for it. When I, a black neurosurgeon and director of the department, walk in and see a family, I must be a messiah. They perceive me as being more powerful than a white physician in the same role. It's just racism in a more benign form.

It's just as important for the white male to train with me as it is for the black woman to train with me. It's important for them both to know that neurosurgery is not the white man's province.

My mother is a role model, because she's bright, energetic, and committed, and has a sense that getting up each day is an adventure. My grandmother is also a role model because she always treated me like I was a person who was worth listening to even when I was a little person and not worth listening to.

I used to tease my parents by saying, "You're raising me to be the person that you don't want my brothers to marry."

People are just not very ambitious for women still. Your son you want to be the best he can be. Your daughter you want to be happy.

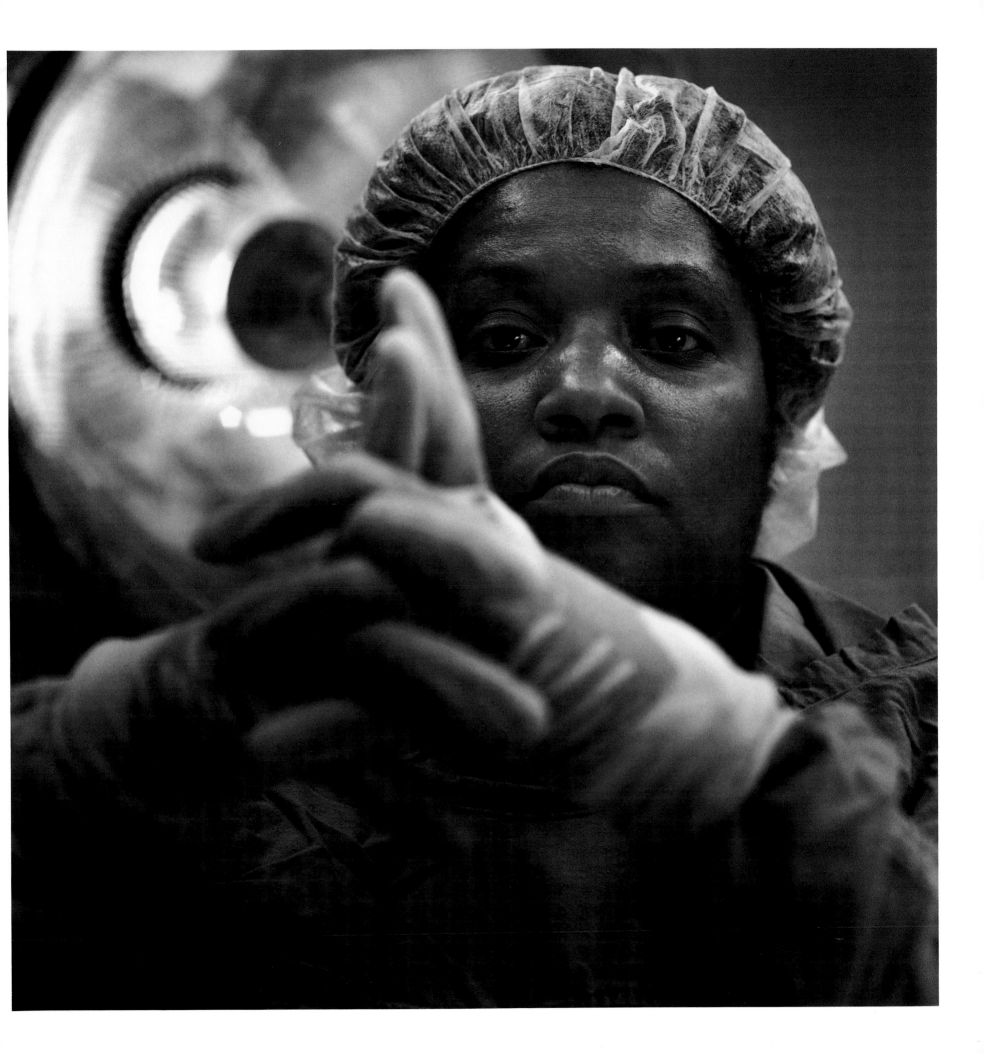

Yvonne Brathwaite Burke

Born October 5, 1932, in Los Angeles, California

I was one of two black girls in the women's honor society at my high school. We were going on a field trip to Popswillow Lake and we had all looked forward to it. When I went to school to meet the bus that Saturday morning, there was no one there except the other girl. We sat and we sat and we sat. Finally we went to her house and her mother called the lake. They said that blacks were not allowed.

I was in the principal's office at eight o'clock Monday morning. "Why would you have me sitting out there all morning?" I asked her. "Why would you do that?" She said, "I just didn't want to hurt your feelings." That probably hurt me the most. I feel it as much today.

When I was in law school at the University of Southern California, there was an instructor who would have Ladies' Day. There were only five women in a class of seventy-five and on Ladies' Day, we would have to recite all day. The reason was that when the first woman graduate from that law school went to court and the judge got hard on her, she cried. And our faculty said, "There'll never be another woman who graduates from this school who is not tough."

When I graduated from law school, there was not a law firm that would even interview me. There were no Jews in major law firms unless they were Jewish firms. There were no women. There were certainly no blacks in major law firms then. So the thing I have that maybe other people don't have is concrete proof that change comes about.

I'm willing to take a chance because I really believe I'm going to win. But you're not going to win unless you try. You know, there was a time I was a picketer across the street. Then I decided I didn't want to be there outside of policy-making. I wanted to be inside, fighting right there on their turf.

I wanted everything. And I decided I wanted a family. I had people who said, "Well, you're in Congress now. You've made these choices in terms of career. You can't do everything." I didn't know that there had never been another woman

in Congress to have a baby. I just assumed there had been.

Certainly, women have achieved more status in business and government. But even if their husbands are very enlightened, women still have the responsibility of the home. When I went into committee meetings I didn't have to wait for statistics on food prices, because when I'd leave Congress I'd stop in the supermarket on my way home.

In the civil rights movement, the people who walked at the front were always women, because traditionally, among blacks, women have been the chance-takers. A disproportionate number of plaintiffs were women. Even the children who integrated the schools were mostly girls. If a black man had sat down on the bus, he would have simply been killed. It's tougher to kill a middle-aged black woman.

In the South, if we had waited to change the hearts and minds of the people, it would have taken two more generations. We don't have time. As far as I'm concerned, you're not going to change the hearts and minds. You have to change the law.

I came along at a time when there was a demand to give men greater visibility and opportunity. In white society they were saying, "Women can't do it." In black society, they were saying, "Women do too much." It's a diabolical situation.

There's still this perception that women are not deal-makers, not tough enough to run major corporations.

There's even more pressure to keep women from moving into the top echelons due to the international dimension of most major business today. If you look at Japan and the Arab world, they are not places where women have access to the top. What do you do about a major oil company that wants to send a woman over to the Middle East to negotiate and she can't even drive a car there?

When I walk into a room I assume I have to prove myself. I know that. I'm accustomed to that. But I also know I *can* prove myself.

When Yvonne Brathwaite Burke was elected to the House of Representatives in 1972, she was the first woman sent to Congress from California in twenty years, and the first black woman ever elected from that state. In 1978, after serving three terms, she returned to California, where she became a specialist in public finance and a partner with the law firm of Jones, Day, Reavis & Pogue. She was recently re-elected to her second four-year term as a Los Angeles County Supervisor for the Second District. She is an L.A. Cares Board member, and a member of the Metropolitan Transportation Authority. She serves on the Board of Directors of the NAACP Legal Defense and Education Fund. Supervisor Burke has received numerous honors and awards; she is a Fellow of Yale University and The Kennedy School of Government at Harvard University, and a recipient of the UCLA 1996 Alumni of the Year award.

Dorothy Irene Height

Born March 24, 1912, in Richmond, Virginia

I participated in impromptu speech contests and I had won a number of prizes for my school, Rankin High [Rankin, Pennsylvania]. When I was a finalist in a state contest, my school principal and my Latin teacher drove me to Harrisburg, the capital, to participate in the final. My mother had hung my dress in the car and said to me, "Dorothy, keep yourself together. No matter what happens, just hold yourself together."

When we got to the hotel, they wouldn't let us in. My teachers didn't know what we were going to do. I said, "Well, I have my dress. And if you could get me some milk and graham crackers, I'll be all right." They were both sort of shattered. But I changed my dress and went into the contest.

I was the last to speak. For my subject I drew the Brighton Peace Compact. In my speech I talked about Woodrow Wilson and the League of Nations. And I said, "What Brighton said was true. We can't have peace just by having the League of Nations nor any other thing. It's in the hearts of people."

Then I said that the message of peace came two thousand years ago. And the messenger could not get into the inn, like I could not get into the hotel that night because I was a Negro. To my surprise, I won the first prize. The irony of this was that they were all white judges.

I joined the staff of the Harlem branch of the YWCA in 1937. One day when Mrs. [Mary McLeod] Bethune was holding a meeting I was asked to be on hand to see that Mrs. Eleanor Roosevelt was ushered into the auditorium. This was at a time when the wife of the President would drive her own roadster and park it on a Harlem street with no Secret Service.

I took her in and she spoke, and when she was leaving, Mrs. Bethune said to me, "What is your name? Come back, we need you." Mrs. Bethune had an uncanny way of getting you involved. She had some very deep spiritual qualities, and she was also an astute organizer and politician.

When I came to Washington, she involved me in the National Council of Negro Women. I became the last volunteer Executive Secretary for the National Council. What I like about what Mrs. Bethune was trying to do was that it was always task-oriented. Drinking tea and wearing white gloves, all that was superficial. The reality was, we were dealing with child labor, minimum wage, and the working conditions of people.

When we wanted to put up a monument to her in the park, we had to go to Congress. Our efforts were interrupted by the civil rights movement, when even our people were saying, "Should you give to a monument or should you give to getting Dr. King out of jail?" You know what the choice was. We had to work through five sessions of Congress and four Presidents to achieve that.

In the 1960s a philanthropic foundation was concerned about what was happening to black America. They brought together Roy Wilkins of the NAACP; Whitney Young of the National Urban League; A. Philip Randolph of the Brotherhood of Sleeping Car Porters; James Farmer of CORE; C. Eric Lincoln, who had done work on the Black Muslims; Martin Luther King, Jr. of SCLC; Jack Greenberg with the NAACP Legal Defense Fund; and me. I represented the concerns of women through the Council.

We had been meeting together over a fourteen-month period when Medgar Evers was assassinated. On the morning that his funeral took place, we had a breakfast meeting with almost a hundred people to discuss the situation. There was some tension between the NAACP and SNCC, a little fear. You could say it was a woman's view, but I remember having to speak up and say that we had to have the young people sitting around the table with us. It was generally agreed that people would use different tactics because we didn't know which one would work. Then John Lewis [of SNCC] became a part of that united civil rights group.

We incorporated ourselves as the United Civil Rights Leadership in order to facilitate support. But there was never any formal president, secretary, or treasurer.

Dr. King always kept things centered on what the goals were. He never let things get competitive. Dr. King had an appreciation of the role that women played in the situation. I was always treated as a peer. It was as good and strong a male-female peer relationship as people would have had at that time in our history.

Black women are the backbone of every institution, but sometimes they are not recognized as even being there, even in the civil rights movement.

There was a myth across the South that the only two free people were the white male and the black woman, and that black women had better chances at jobs. Well, that was because they scrubbed floors.

We've got to work to save our children and do it with full respect for the fact that if we do not, no one else is going to do it. We're not going to allow ourselves to be told that we cannot function, that we dysfunction.

Frederick Douglass said, "In the struggle for justice, the only reward is the opportunity to be in the struggle." You can't expect that you're going to have it tomorrow. You just have to keep working on it.

Dorothy Height has been the president of the National Council of Negro Women since 1957. The Council, founded in 1935 by Mary McLeod Bethune, is a coalition of over thirty organizations representing four million women. Ms. Height earned a bachelor's and a master's degree in social work from New York University. After a career of thirty-three years with the YWCA, she retired in 1977. In 1993, she was presented with the NAACP's Springarn Medal. The year 1996 saw the birth of the Dorothy I. Height Leadership Institute.

Dorothy Height organized the drive to erect a statue of Mary McLeod Bethune, which became the first monument to a black American in a public park in Washington, D.C.

Sarah Vaughan

Born March 27, 1924, in Newark, New Jersey
Died April 3, 1990, in Beverly Hills, California

From sassy to sublime, Sarah Vaughan sang her way into the hearts of millions around the world. When she started performing in the 1940s, critics and fans agreed that she was one of the most inspired and original singers to appear since the great Ella Fitzgerald. She recorded jazz and popular songs, transforming standards into stylish signature pieces whether with small ensembles, big bands, or fifty-piece orchestras. She won numerous music polls and continued to perform and record until her death in 1990.

How do you find you sing? Just like I found out I could walk, I guess. I mostly played piano and organ in church. Nobody knew I could sing, because I was the piano player.

In the back of my mind I always wanted to be in show business. I did the Apollo Amateur Hour [in 1942] just to get the ten-dollar first prize. I didn't think I was going to win. But I won and got a week performing at the theater. That week Ella Fitzgerald was the star attraction on the bill. I know how lucky I was to be there with her. And voom, in about two weeks, I was in show business. I was singing with Earl "Fatha" Hines and Billy Eckstine at the age of eighteen.

My first record was with Billy Eckstine in 1945 or 1946. The name of the song was "I'll Wait and Pray." I didn't wait. I prayed right away.

I thought I'd just be in show business for a hot minute. But it's been forty-six years.

God is good, that's what I'll say. I never took lessons. Being with Billy Eckstine's band, being with Earl Hines's band, the fellas taught me everything I knew. We all taught each other, we all learned from each other. In fact, I'm still learning.

I listen to horn players more than I do singers. They play more music. I sing what they play, not everything, but I get ideas from them. Dizzy Gillespie, Charlie Parker, Gene Ammons, my goodness! I've worked with those guys. How fortunate!

Charlie Parker was fantastic, a genius on that horn, a genius music-wise. He used to sit on the bus or train with Stravinsky scores. And then he'd get on the stage and play something from Stravinsky, but play it his way. Nobody ever knew that.

There's no end to music. Another generation comes along with something else, and I'm a big copycat. You won't know it, but I am.

I listen to all singers. Leontyne Price is my favorite singer.

I have lots of favorite singers. Marian Anderson, Stevie Wonder. I'd like to sing with Leontyne Price. I'd like to sing with the tenor from Italy [Luciano Pavarotti]. There's a lot of people I'd love to sing with, singers that can sing.

I just sing. I don't know what I sound like or who I sound like. I don't know what kind of singer I am. I just open my mouth and sing.

If I was coming into show business now, what would I be coming into? I'd have to be a rock 'n' roll singer. I don't think I'd make it.

Practice? When I'm on stage, that's it. When I want to learn a new song, we have rehearsals, but that's it. It's different every time. Singing a song the same way for the rest of your life is quite boring.

I really love this business. The bad goes with it. If it's all good, it's no good.

I'm not an amen, amen, amen-ing person, but I'm a religious person.

We'd be gone on the road for three or four months before we'd get back to New York. We'd have fun on the buses. We used to get pots and pans and cook in the rooms where you're not supposed to. You smoke cigars to keep the odor down.

I'm slowing down because I'm getting sick of the road. I pick my places now. It took a long time to be able to do that. Twenty years ago, I said, "Where's the work?" If anybody had told me then that I'd be off for three months, I'd have said you've got to be kidding, I'd starve to death. But after forty-six years, I saved my money pretty well.

When I'm off the road, I like to travel, just go where I like. I like to ride trains. When I can do what I want to do in this business, then I'm a star. Not the glamor part.

Show business is not the easiest thing to get into, but if that's what you want, you've got to stick with it. A lot of times, I wanted to go home to Mama. There's been thrills and chills, and ups and downs ever since I've been in show business. It never stops.

Josephine Riley Matthews

Born October 3, 1897, in Aiken Country, South Carolina
Died December 14, 1993, in Wagoner, South Carolina

During four decades as a licensed midwife, Mama Jo safely delivered more than 1,300 babies, black and white, in rural South Carolina. She graduated from high school at age seventy-four. In 1976 the state named her Woman of the Year and Outstanding Older American.

I am the fourth. My great-grandmother was a midwife, my grandmother was a midwife, my mother was a midwife, and then it dropped down into my lap.

I didn't have any children. I am not a birth mother.

As far as I know, two or three women have said they waited on themselves, they would get everything ready and deliver their babies, tie and cut the cord and go on. But I know it is a hard job. To be able to help the mothers and the babies, it was a pleasure. Before I left home on a labor case, or if I had to leave in a rush, I would ask the Lord to go with me to help me do this delivery and it seems like it just opened the way.

There was one, she was supposed to go to the doctor and she didn't go. I said I am not going to deliver this baby but I will take you to the hospital and I took her in my car and started to the Lexington hospital. I had stopped to get some gasoline on the road. We were, I reckon, about five miles from Lexington and she said, ''This baby's coming.'' I said, ''Well, you have to take care of that 'cause I got to handle this wheel.'' She didn't have a bit of trouble.

I had one father that just about passed out. I said, ''Go to the kitchen and bring me that kettle of hot water.'' So he come back just shaking, shaking. His aunt was there. I told her, ''You take him.'' She put him on the bed so he didn't know when that baby come. The mother, she was doing all right. He's the one that fainted.

The funniest thing happened. The baby was about a year old and I was passing that way and I said I'm going to stop in here and see this baby. The oldest little boy was about four years old, I reckon, and there were two under him, and the baby. When I got there he was taking care of the baby. The four-year-old said, ''Miss Josephine,'' he said, ''now we want this one but don't bring no more them babies here. We'll keep this one, but don't bring no more in that little black bag.'' The parent was telling I brought the babies in a bag. The way he said it and the way he looked, he wasn't joking.

I was supposed to retire when I was seventy-two years old, but I was seventy-seven when I retired. On my seventy-sixth birthday a lady had triplets. It was quite a birthday present.

Well, the Bible says the strong should bear the infirmities of the weak. So the woman is supposed to be the weaker sex, but they sure have to stand up for the men a lot of times. I'll bet you one thing, if the man had to have the first baby there wouldn't be but two in the family. Yes sir, let him have the first one and the woman the next one, and his time wouldn't come around no more.

Niara Sudarkasa

Born August 14, 1938, in Fort Lauderdale, Florida

I grew up as a West Indian. There was never any question that I was a black American, but in Florida people would call me "a Nassau" because my grandparents were from the Bahamas and they were the ones with whom I lived.

We had a very big family. My grandmother was one of twenty children. They all had big families so I grew up thinking that every second person I'd meet would be a cousin.

When I went to Oberlin, I took a course on Caribbean cultures and came across a reference to *esusu* or *esu*, which are savings associations in Haiti and Jamaica and almost every part of the Caribbean. An article by a student of the Yoruba in Nigeria described esu as a Yoruba credit association. I believe that was the beginning of my determination to study Africa, because I had known about esu from childhood. Instead of using banks or post offices, these Bahamians used esu. I felt thrilled because for the first time I really did concretely understand that there was a cultural link to Africa. I determined that I would go to West Africa to learn more about the history of the area from which we came. That's how I came to begin this long-term association with the continent that I have had.

[In Africa], I felt for the first time what it meant to be a majority person. What struck me about the small Yoruba town I lived in were the similarities to things I knew as a child. There were postures, the way they did things. The fact that women were the market traders and had a life-style that made them very independent. There were no housewives among these women. This was something that I recognized.

I think that being in Nigeria in the early sixties increased my sense of pride in the African heritage. I felt that we were all one people with a destiny that was very much interwoven.

I didn't come away feeling that home is only in America and Nigeria is another country. I felt definitely and deeply that this was a part of me.

Fort Lauderdale never belonged to me. I was always conscious that this was not mine. There was always that hand above us, people in control who intruded in our lives from time to time. I felt that it was my country but not my land.

But when I went to West Africa, I had the deep sense not only of belonging, but of possession. This was ours! The whole continent was ours!

Africans belie every stereotype about blacks. I'm impressed with how smart they are and I feel very hopeful because Africans have the intelligence, ingenuity, and now the training to make this one of the great continents technologically, economically, and so on. As Ali Mazrui and others have said, "Africa is the world's richest continent with the poorest people." It's one of the great ironies of the twentieth century.

I wanted to affirm an association with the continent by taking another name. It was a political decision that some black Americans were making. Sudarkasa came by marriage. The word *nia* in Swahili means purpose. So Niara was an adaptation and the name was given to me to mean a woman of high purpose.

I didn't change my name because I didn't like it, or because I wanted to reject it as a slave name. Legally I'm still Gloria Marshall Clark and Niara Sudarkasa. My passport has both.

At the University of Michigan, I was a part of the establishment. But I was very politicized about Africa so I was a vocal spokesperson for all the things that the students were advocating in those days, the early seventies: black studies, more black and minority students in the university. At Michigan I became the activist I had not been in the sixties, and most people knew me there as an activist-scholar.

I was devoted to Malcolm X. I admired Martin Luther King but I thought Malcolm's analysis of the black condition was in many cases more apt, more accurate than King's. I think he understood that love was not going to conquer all and that this was a confrontation over power.

I think that I bring to the study of Africa a concern for the way Africans look at their cultures that many European and white American scholars don't have. I also think I bring a respect for Africa that is important if one is going to give a picture of the continent that is balanced.

At Lincoln, which had a long and very distinguished tradition of association with African institutions and the continent, I feel that I'm in the best possible position I could be. It's a specially ordained appointment, because I don't think there is any other African-American institution of higher education that has had such a close tie to the continent.

Lincoln was one of the best institutions of higher learning in this country at the beginning of the twentieth century. I want it to be one of the best at the beginning of the twenty-first century. We owe blacks the same opportunity for higher education that others have. And I think that black colleges are the primary vehicles for providing that.

Niara Sudarkasa is the first woman president of Lincoln University, the nation's oldest black college, and a formerly all-male institution. Prior to her appointment at Lincoln in 1987, she was the associate vice-president for academic affairs at the University of Michigan at Ann Arbor, where she was the first black woman to receive tenure. Dr. Sudarkasa's most recent book, The Strength of Our Mothers *(1996) is a collection of essays on African and African American women and families. She has received four White House appointments, including the 1993 appointment to the White House Commission on Presidential Scholars, made by President Clinton.*

Wilma Rudolph

Born June 23, 1940, in Clarksville, Tennessee
Died November 12, 1994, Brentwood, Tennessee

Wilma Rudolph was the first American woman to win three gold medals in track and field at a single Olympiad. A bronze medalist at the 1956 Olympics in Melbourne, she won the 100-meter and 200 meter sprints and then ran the anchor leg for the United States 4 x 100 relay-winning team in 1960 in Rome; she set world records in all three events. She has been inducted into the Women's Sports Hall of Fame, the Black Sports Hall of Fame, the U.S. Olympic Hall of Fame, and the National Women's Hall of Fame. Her autobiography, Wilma, *was published in 1977 and adapted for a television movie, which starred Cicely Tyson. A teacher, coach, and advocate for youth, she spent her remaining years as president of the Indianapolis-based Wilma Rudolph Foundation, which she created for the training of young athletes.*

I was safe by the time I was twelve, but it was hard for me to remember all of those terrible days before then. I had a series of childhood illnesses. It started off as scarlet fever and from there it was polio.

My father was the one who sort of babied me and was sympathetic. He was a determined person. He had to be. There were twenty-two children. I am the twentieth. My mother was the one who made me work, made me believe that one day it would be possible for me to walk without braces.

They would take me to a doctor at Meharry Medical College in Nashville, Tennessee, and when we got back home, they would show everybody the massages and exercises that I did when I was in the hospital. It got to the point where everybody could basically share in the exercises, so we used to make a game out of it. When my parents were gone, I would take the braces off and walk around. I think by doing that I probably walked a lot sooner than I would have.

I didn't like any of my friends. Your peers are always the worst. They tease you or if you are playing a game, nobody wants to hold your hand because you have a brace on. I used to hate that. I think my way of getting back at them was through a sport. That was also a form of motivation and determination.

Around nine the braces came off and now I can't remember which leg I wore my braces on. The next thing I knew I was normal. I was doing everything that everyone else could do. Once I discovered I could run, I spent all of my extra time running.

I was six feet, eighty-nine pounds, and I wanted to be the greatest basketball player that ever came through my tiny high school. My coach said the way I buzzed around so irritated him that he called me "Mosquito." As I grew older, they dropped the first portion and everybody I know calls me "Skeeter."

When the basketball season is over kids are always looking for another sport. You don't want to go home in the afternoon to do chores. So there was my motivation for track and field.

[In college] our coach always protected us. Places he knew we could not use the bathroom, he didn't take us. It made it easier to accomplish something, to be proud and not have to mix any world affairs that we couldn't solve with the accomplishment.

Coming from this small southern town, I was always determined that I was never going to stay there and not see the rest of the world. When I went to my first Olympics in Melbourne, Australia [1956], I was a green sixteen-year-old, innocent and naive.

After winning the bronze medal in the 4 × 100 relay, the most difficult thing was going back and getting very angry inside about how people perceived black people where I lived. That's when you rebel.

I worked very hard for the next four years. In Rome, I was self-motivated, motivated by my family. It took sheer determination to be able to run a hundred yards and remember all of the mechanics that go along with it. It takes steady nerves and being a fighter to stay out there.

From the moment you walk into the stadium, you block out everything and everybody, until you get the command to start. I could only hear the cheers after the race was over.

After 1960, of course, everything changed. When I got back from the Olympics, my hometown, which had never been integrated, decided to have a parade for me. I told them that I could not come to a parade that would be segregated. So, I sort of broke that barrier in my hometown. I probably did everything that I wasn't supposed to do, but it was to pave the way for other blacks in the town.

Sometimes it takes years to really grasp what has happened to your life. What do you do after you are world-famous and nineteen or twenty and you have sat with prime ministers, kings and queens, the Pope? What do you do after that? Do you go back home and take a job? What do you do to keep your sanity? You come back to the real world.

I wanted to make more money than I knew other women made. But there was no place for a black woman to make money in the world of advertising and marketing. We know why.

If you listen to everybody else you will feel sorry for yourself, because they will say, "If you had been white, you would have been a millionaire." What kind of answer do you expect me to give you? I am not white. I am a black woman and that is the bottom line.

When I was going through my transition of being famous, I used to ask God, why was I here? what was my purpose? Surely, it wasn't just to win three gold medals. There has to be more to this life than that.

I would be very disappointed if I were only remembered as a runner because I feel that my contribution to the youth of America has far exceeded the woman who was the Olympic champion. The challenge is still there.

Odetta

Born December 31, 1930, in Birmingham, Alabama

Odetta helped to bring folksongs out of the archives and backwoods and into the mainstream of popular American culture. Using her music to speak on political issues, she has performed at civil rights demonstrations and peace rallies, including the March on Washington in 1963. Work songs, freedom and prison songs, spirituals, ballads, and blues are part of a repertoire she sings around the world. She traveled to Beijing, China, in 1996 as an elder attending the International Women's Conference. Odetta: Ballads and Blues was re-issued in 1996, and Odetta: To Ella was released in 1998. The year 1999 marks her 50th anniversary in show business.

Generally, most kids are humanists. They think about what's fair and not fair. I was one of those, too, and slavery didn't seem fair. I learned a very biased and excluding history. I was learning that the slaves were happy and singing all the time. I was ashamed.

It wasn't till getting into the folk music—reading the histories that came from the people the music was collected from—that I found out the strength of what we come from, the determination on living, finding ways of getting over, around, or through. I mean, to the point where no one in my earshot can denigrate Aunt Jemima or Uncle Tom. They did things, in order to get us someplace, that I'm sure I wouldn't have the strength to do.

Folk music is where I live.

I'm not saying that Los Angeles [where my family moved when I was six] was Utopia. But I would have turned out another person had I grown up in Birmingham, Alabama, where we had those deafening signs that kept telling you you were not quite right.

At the age of thirteen, I started taking voice lessons seriously. I was taking piano lessons and we were waiting for the piano teacher, seeing how high we could sing. When the piano teacher got in, she checked our voices and she took me on as a voice student. I was a coloratura soprano. It was very high.

I would sing at recitals and at churches. The minister at these things would probably be dozing off, and if I was singing, I would go up real high and wake him up. As I remember it, there was always a fascination with high tones or high voices within the black church.

I adored Marian Anderson. She is an absolute model for me, has always been. But even in those days, shy and backward and afraid of every single thing as I was, somehow that extra whatever it is we come into the world with knew that you can't be another person.

I had no clue that I would be able to earn my living with singing. I didn't have that kind of crystal ball going. I was dedicated to the music. I needed the music. I needed to study. I needed to play my three chords and sing "On Top of Old Smokey," or whatever other song I was learning.

I was loaned a guitar that was strung with steel strings and it may as well have been barbed wire. I call my guitar "Chumpy Chump." It's a rhythm guitar, sufficient for what I'm doing. When guitarists admire what I do on the guitar, I say, "It's self-defense."

Paul Robeson politicized me. He was the one that helped me realize that it was not only possible, but necessary, to turn around and be helpful to your brothers and sisters. I remember the era when someone black did a spectacular thing, it soothed, made us proud, the whole of the black community.

Folk music straightened my back and it kinked my hair. What is an Afro or natural today used to be called an Odetta.

In those days—late fifties, early sixties—I was singing on sheer unadulterated hate. I hated myself and everybody else and everything else. First of all, they lied to me about my forebears being happy and singing all the time. Then, whenever we saw ourselves in the movies, it was in subservient roles, stereotype roles. Whenever Africa was depicted in the movies, it was shameful. You just wanted a hole to open up for you to sink down in.

Earlier on, I was attracted to the prison songs, and through them I could get my hate off. No one knew where I ended and the prisoner began. So I hid in that music. I could get away with the hate.

The time of the civil rights movement was very interesting. There were a lot of things, people in different places, just smoldering. As I was singing, I was one of those things that was smoldering, and so it all miraculously came together.

I like being useful. I like what I do to be able to help someone. I called it helping, to keep up the spirit of those who were on the actual firing lines. I'm not quite sure why educating and entertaining have to be separated.

The March on Washington was a great day in my life. I was stunned and overwhelmed and it filled me with joy. The greatness of that day was seeing all those people there, all my folks there. Especially when there is, somewhere in the ether, the notion that we can't stick together. I saw that one knocked right out of the box.

No one can dub you with dignity. That's yours to claim.

My feeling is, the better we feel about ourselves, the fewer times we have to knock somebody down in order to stand on top of their bodies and feel tall.

This nation is like a teenage nation among old and ancient nations. But it is possible to rewrite the books at this time. We are living at an exciting time in a nation where we can stir it up. This is the place.

Cora Lee Johnson

Born December 12, 1925, in Soperton, Georgia

Cora Lee Johnson is a social activist who was recognized by a national magazine as a "hero for hard times." She began working in the fields when she was eight years old. After she learned about government services available to poor people through the Georgia Legal Services program, she pressured for—and achieved—changes, especially in housing, health, and nutrition. She chairs the Treutlen County Client Council and the Rural Black Women's Leadership Project. Recent recognition of her work has included the "Women Who Dared" Award, presented by the National Black Women's Health Project in 1994; the National Advocate of the Year Award, from Oxfam America in 1996; and the Voices of Vision Award, presented by Glory Foods and the National Council of Negro Women in 1998.

I dropped out of school when I was about thirteen, still in the fourth grade. I got married on the second Sunday in October in 1940, and went to the field to pull corn that Monday. So I come out of one cornfield into another. I just changed fields and changed names, but I didn't change anything else.

I had got pregnant one time, but I lost the baby. I didn't know I was pregnant. Cutting wood and hauling wood, the doctor say that's what caused me to lose it, lifting the big logs and stuff.

The hard time that I had coming up to where I am now helped me in a lot of ways to be strong, 'cause I didn't have nobody to depend on for strength but God and myself. And I didn't have much confidence in myself.

I know I fight a lot of losing battles and I do a lot of unnecessary things that—if I had the education—I wouldn't have to do. So I have to go the long way around. But one thing about it, once I make that long trip I been there and I don't have to go back and make up all the little things I skipped over.

I created my own self a job. I don't have any education. I can't even read the pattern, but I can sew it. I saw that uneducated peoples could do this. I don't only teach old peoples. I have young peoples, too.

Nothing is free. Like these little programs that the government got, sayin' it's free. It costs you your everything. 'Cause once you go in to get food stamps or a welfare check, if you had any secret, you don't have it when you leave there.

I played Lazarus too long, stayed under the table and never got nothin' but the crumbs. I want to eat the rest of the while that I'm here. So then I got to get out from under the table. If the meat on top of the table, then you got to stand up where it is.

I was trying to find out why the people wasn't getting their food stamps. The black was afraid to go to the whites and ask for it. This place here is a place that you was always told what to do, when to do it, and how to do it.

If you ain't got, you ain't got, I don't care what color you is. Those people that have the money treat all of us the same way, and maybe treats some of them worser 'cause some of them won't shake the bushes like some of us will.

People was being turned down for food stamps for all kinds of reasons. I tried to talk to the director and couldn't get through to her. But I learned in this training, everybody got a boss man. So if I can't talk to you, I talk to your boss man. You got boss mans all the way from here to Washington. And I'll go and talk to them boss mans too if I can't talk to none in between here and Washington.

Some said all I was going to do was create a problem for the people that lived in Soperton. I told them you didn't have to create nothin', just live here and it was a problem.

Public housing, health issues, whatever issues the poor people have, I works with it. I sets on eight different boards and all that is voluntary. They don't pay me to set on none of it. So then they can't fire me 'cause they ain't got me hired. So at least you have that much freedom to say what you want to say.

One thing what makes fear is power. I don't have anything that they can take and I'm not afraid of losing nothing, 'cause you can't lose something you don't have. I lost my health, I lost my husband, I lost my house, I lost my furniture. I never had a reputation 'cause I always been a troublemaker, so I didn't lose that.

One doctor said he didn't believe that I was as sick as I say I was. He'd draw blood every time and my blood didn't show him that I had a back problem. And I told him it wasn't my blood that was hurting. It was my back that was hurting.

I was trying to get a birth certificate and I got a letter that said that Cora Lee Walker did not exist. So I was walkin' around here and wasn't here. So everything that can happen to you have happened, including not bein' here.

I am a person. I have feelings. I have needs. I have wants. I'm sittin' here and nobody sees me. Everybody just looks over me and walks on past because I'm black, because I'm a woman, because I'm poor, because I have no education. But I'm still here.

We have come a long ways since I started. We have three black city councilmen, which had never happened in the history of Soperton. No black have ever set on nothin' but a chair.

I won't give up. Nobody will have the chance to say, "Well, she got tired of it and she give up." They won't be able to say that. I get tired, and I go home, and I cry, and I read, get some more strength while I'm sleepin' and get up in the morning and come out again.

I have been invited everywhere to make speeches. I think people admire me for being the voice for the peoples that won't speak for theirself. I don't fear what they might do to me 'cause they about done everything but killt me and I think God's got control of that.

Eleanor Holmes Norton

Born June 13, 1937, in Washington, D.C.

I'm a fourth-generation Washingtonian. I'm the oldest of three girls. Although I am not three years older than the third child, I was treated as if more was expected of me and therefore I internalized a sense of striving and responsibility.

"Middle class" has to be understood as a cultural phenomenon in the black community. Many people had a striving mentality. Even though they worked in white folks' kitchens or their fathers were laborers, there was a cultural striving that would separate them from people—white or black—who conceived of themselves as being in their proper place.

Blacks did not define their place by their work, or else all of us would have had to define ourselves as down-and-out. So you defined yourself by who you thought yourself to be.

I was raised to think that when you couldn't go to the white schools that those whites were poor white trash anyway. You felt superior to those who kept you from those schools.

Black children were raised, not simply by their parents, but by their neighborhoods. It was a set of institutions and the way they meshed. A lot of black children don't have that today. Today the church is not at the center of black culture. The school is beleaguered and much criticized. And the neighborhood—certainly for inner-city children—is often a part of the problem, rather than the solution.

When the majority of black children are being born to single women, family obviously does not play the role it played. It must once again do that, because you can't remain a whole and viable people if children are raised essentially only by women. I think it's the most important problem confronting the black community.

In college it was very hard to decide what to do. My contentiousness, the gusto with which the adversarial struck me as a way to proceed, especially in the age of segregation when there was a lot to be adversarial about, made me want to be a civil rights lawyer.

When I went to law school, I got a master's degree in American history and a law degree at the same time, for no reason except that you want to stretch your mind.

My conception of myself was entirely existential. You keep reaching, you don't know quite where it will lead, so you are involved in the reaching for its own sake.

You could say race was an obstacle to me, you could say sex was an obstacle to me, but I refused to own them in that way. I was black and female, but I never conceived that those were supposed to keep me from doing what I wanted to do.

I have not been animated in my life to fight against race and sex discrimination simply because of my own identity.

That would mean that one must be South African to fight apartheid, or a poor white in Appalachia to fight poverty, or Jewish to fight anti-Semitism. And I just reject that conception of how struggles should be waged.

One ought to struggle for its own sake. One ought to be against racism and sexism because they are wrong, not because one is black or one is female.

Black people get their moral authority in this country not simply because they have suffered, but because they understand the suffering of other people in this world.

In every society in the world, being female has limitations on one's self-development. The untold billions of women who could paint and write and speak and do all the things men do, that's never to be recovered. That's lost to the world.

American business increasingly understands that there's no place to get the talent from anymore. This understanding may, ultimately, do as much to liberate women and blacks as the antidiscrimination measures. The need for their talent in a country where birthrates are declining and talent needs accelerating is irresistible.

The country has suffered too much from its failure, generation after generation, to take on race, deal with it, and finally set it aside.

Most people who know me would speak of my passion. But I pride myself as well on the ability to think coldly through a problem. In the middle of a revolution, you don't want somebody who is just going to go out there and raise a flag and say, "Follow me." You want somebody who has figured out how to get through this battle.

It was not difficult for me as an ACLU lawyer to represent people with whom I had profound disagreements, such as George Wallace. Because of the nature of struggle, you end up representing people on the left 99 percent of the time. Therefore you love it when you get to make the point through someone with whom you patently disagree.

There's no way to argue, nor should there be, that black people ought to have freedom of speech and racists shouldn't. If the principle is going to live at all, it's got to live for anybody who wants to exercise it.

I think the Constitution is one of the great documents in the world. How has it survived two hundred years? Because it's not what it was. We ought to look at the Constitution through its metamorphosis—from a document that denied the personhood of black people and denied the political reality of women, to a document that has, in part through war and struggle, come to encompass them and others.

Eleanor Holmes Norton was the first woman to chair the Equal Employment Opportunity Commission; she served during the Carter Administration from 1977 to 1981. A constitutional and civil rights lawyer, she worked with the American Civil Liberties Union before being appointed to head the New York City Commission on Human Rights in 1970. She is a graduate of Antioch College and Yale University, and has been a professor at the Georgetown University Law Center since 1982. In 1991, Holmes Norton was elected non-voting delegate to the U.S. Congress, representing the District of Columbia. She was reelected in 1994 with 87 percent of the vote. In 1993, for the first time since the District's creation in 1790, she brought a debate and vote on statehood to the floor of the House of Representatives. Although the vote was lost, her efforts dramatized the problems of the nation's capital.

Ophelia DeVore-Mitchell

Born August 12, 1923, in Edgefield, South Carolina

Ophelia DeVore-Mitchell paved the way for models of color when she founded the Grace Del Marco Model Agency and the Ophelia DeVore School of Self-Development and Modeling in New York City in the late 1940s. Branching out from modeling, she became a marketing consultant and in the 1960s created a line of cosmetics. She is the publisher of The Columbus Times, *a weekly newspaper in Columbus, Georgia, and has added DeVore-Carter Communications to her core organization in order to serve the broader needs of working women in our changing society. In 1996, the National Association of Negro Business & Professional Women recognized DeVore-Mitchell and* The Columbus Times *for Dedicated Service to the Community, and she herself received the "Breaking the Mold Award" for Pioneering the Development of Economic Development for Black Women, presented by Professional Women of Color in 1997.*

Because of my family's complexion and background [Indian, French, and African], we were kind of in the middle. Sometimes we were fighting with the whites, and then sometimes we were fighting with the blacks. Sometimes you didn't know where you fit in.

I went to the Vogue Modeling School in New York. I got excellent training. They didn't know I was black. They didn't know what I was. But I didn't know they didn't know, because I knew what I was, why shouldn't they?

I went to modeling school because I wanted to be in show business. But my parents said that only bad girls went into show business. At that time, modeling was so young, it had no kind of reputation. So it was acceptable to my parents.

When I first started in the modeling business, the only whites accepted as models to represent the image of America were the Nordics. The Mediterranean Europeans could not be a part of it.

I'm not really the first black model, although I'd say I was one of the first who had been thoroughly trained and had a good background in the business. I was one of the first ones to go down Seventh Avenue and Broadway and get clothes for the models. They didn't give clothes to black models. They thought all black models worked in somebody's home or something.

Blacks were being presented as stereotypes, like Aunt Jemima or Uncle Tom images. I didn't model a long time, because that wasn't my mission, to be a model. My mission was to have us presented in a way that was not stereotyped.

So five of us got together and started an agency. When we went to get the license for the agency, the commissioner said, "There's no demand for black models." So we said, "Well, we'll create a demand." When we started, we found out the women were not trained. Then I had to open a school to train them.

Diahann Carroll was my receptionist at one time. She was only sixteen and she went on a television contest, *Chance of a Lifetime*. Whoever got the most applause won. We got all the tickets we could get, zillions of tickets, and we jammed the place with people for Diahann. Everybody was applauding, and that old meter jumped. These are the things you had to do to get over. A little sneaky maybe, but I didn't set up the criteria. I just dealt with the situation.

We are in the business of selling talent. We are not in the meat business. I made sure that people would attain the things in life they wanted through their merit, rather than through looking at the ceiling.

The whole idea is that I'm trying to give a true picture of what blacks are like. In addition to that, I'm trying to help companies that want to communicate effectively with the black consumer marketplace, and give blacks jobs and bring them into the corporations.

I became a marketing consultant to the advertising industry. They were looking for people to help them to integrate their commercials, products, and promotions and just help them get through the turbulent period of the civil rights movement.

A lot of whites claimed to be knowledgeable, but all they did was confuse the industry. The decision-makers still do not want to give blacks the benefit of the doubt about knowing their people.

In the beginning it was strictly modeling. But then we found out that most blacks and minorities did not necessarily want to be models. What they wanted was recognition as attractive human beings who can do a job in any field.

When I came along, you couldn't have a child in my glamor profession. I wanted five children. What did I do? I had five children. And I never stopped anything.

Just because you get older doesn't mean you get uglier or dodo-ish, and this is what women need to know.

There is not a black agency in the entertainment industry today that is owned by blacks. Years ago, there were loads of them. Once the white agencies found out they could make money on black entertainers, they put pressure on and put every black agency out of business.

I've been in communications all my life. Another extension of what I do is publish the news. I'm one of the founders of the black press archives at Howard University in Washington, D.C. We've got to write our history in reference to the positiveness, because you can't love yourself unless you know that somebody that looks like you has done something good.

Sherian Grace Cadoria

Born January 26, 1940, in Marksville, Louisiana

In 1990, Brigadier General Sherian Grace Cadoria retired from the army after twenty-nine years of outstanding service. At the time the highest-ranking black woman in the United States armed forces, she was one of only four female army generals. She served in Vietnam from January 1967 to October 1969, and held key assignments with the Joint Chiefs of Staff, the Law Enforcement Division, and the Criminal Investigation Command. She was promoted to Brigadier General in 1985. Her military decorations and awards include the Distinguished Service Medal, the Legion of Merit, the Bronze Star with two Oak Leaf Clusters, the Meritorious Service Medal, and the Defense Superior Service Medal. Now president of Cadoria Speaker and Consultancy Service, in 1996, she became "Volunteer Principal" of the Holy Ghost Catholic School in Marksville, Louisiana. Cadoria's own alma mater, it is housed in a one-room building. When the parish priest called for help, she took on the project of the school's rehabilitation.

When we lived in the country, we walked to school. It was five miles to school and five miles home. The bus would pass in front of the house but blacks did not ride the bus. We didn't even think of it.

My mother is a very strong lady with strong moral values. Let me give you an instance. My brother, sister, and I were almost always together because my mom worked. We had to stay together to look after each other. Once we had gone shopping and somebody gave us a penny too much and we brought it home. My mother made the three of us walk back and return it. Remember, town is five miles away. She said that at least one out of the three should have known better, and since we didn't, all three were punished.

Let me tell you, you don't forget lessons like that. I didn't have problems in the military with discipline because my mom really was a first sergeant.

During my junior year at Southern University [in Baton Rouge, Louisiana], this WAC [Women's Army Corps] recruiter came to the campus. Everybody knew I wanted to join the Navy like my brother, but I was selected to represent the university at the College Junior Program. And I spent four weeks at Fort McClellan, in the summer of 1960, training and seeing what enlisted life was like. It was so difficult. It was tough, it was awful. But it was also fascinating to see the jobs and responsibilities these young lieutenants had.

Practically everywhere I go I have more than one job. I used to think, "Well, they only do that because I'm the only little black one, so they pick on me." But I'm very happy that this was done because I had jobs that women did not typically do. And I'd do them all.

Practically every job that I've gone into was a first. Once you do it well, they'll accept someone else.

In Vietnam I interviewed for a protocol job. When I got there, the colonel told me I couldn't do the job. He said, "You can't travel, you can't carry luggage, it's too heavy. Women can't do this." And I said, "Nobody said I couldn't carry those hundred-pound bags of cotton when I was just a little child."

I've gotten more pressure from being female in a man's world than from being black. I was always a role model. I had responsibility not just for black women but for black men, too.

We could only work in the administrative area and nursing. In 1974, women were integrated into the other branches of the army. By law, women cannot participate in combat.

I think society knows that women can function in combat. What it takes is training. There is a type of machoism connected to combat, but there is no mystique to it. You had women Viet Cong.

I really don't want men in combat and I definitely don't want women in combat. It's demoralizing, it's degrading, and it is everything bad. We're not put on this earth to kill one another.

Now on the other side of the picture, let me say that in any field where you have a door shut, you're not allowing a person to exercise their ability. Both in civilian society as well as the military, if you have jobs, then open them up.

If there is ever another world war, you're going to have women POWs. It's going to be a fluid battlefield.

In Vietnam, there were no lines. Although we were very limited in what we were doing, women served in a totally hostile zone.

When I came back from Vietnam, I intended to get out of the military and go into the convent. I think it was the impact of being there as long as I was, over thirty-three months.

But then, in December 1969, the list for Commanding General Staff College was released and I got a call from the director of the Women's Army Corps congratulating me on my selection. "But Colonel," I said, "I'm not going. I'm getting out. I'm going to be a nun."

And she said, "No you're not. Call your mother."

And I did. And she said, "Here you are the first selected to this. You have a responsibility to all blacks to stay in."

A woman today has to do more than her male counterpart. Come in knowing that you're going to have to give 200 percent effort to get 100 percent credit. And most of the time, you will not get 100 percent credit.

I love the military even with all the hardships. When you become a general, and you're female and black, you're going to get some scars. But don't let that turn you off.

There were many nights that I went home and cried. But you do that in your room. You do not do it in front of anyone, ever. No matter what, you don't shed a tear. But when the shower is going, you can let the tears fall.

By act of Congress, male officers are gentlemen, but by act of God, we are ladies. We don't have to be little mini-men and try to be masculine and use obscene language to come across. I can take you and flip you on the floor and put your arms behind your back and you'll never move again, without your ever knowing that I can do it.

Priscilla L. Williams

Born October 10, 1897, in Oakwood, Texas
Died April 16, 1987, in Oklahoma City, Oklahoma

Priscilla Williams was the mother of fourteen children, although she gave birth to none. Her life of hard work and dedication to the family is typical of the lives of many unsung heroines. Celebrating her life, its great and small achievements, is a way of celebrating them all.

Mama and my brother and me, we lived out on a farm. After we picked cotton, the only work the man that owned the farm had was cutting cordwood and splitting rails and making railroad ties. He would always give Mama more than he did the men. She could really cut wood. We'd be sawing that wood and she'd be splitting it.

My daddy, he left me when I was two days old. He ran off with another woman and Mama was sick in bed with me. I didn't see him again until I was about two or three years old. Then one day he passed the house hauling cotton. Mama said I hollered, told Daddy to come over and bring me some candy. And Daddy just popped the whip on the mules, rode on off, and never did look back. And I didn't see my daddy no more until I was thirty-five years old.

Mama would always find some place to sharecrop. Fifty cents a day is what she was getting for chopping cotton and corn, plowing, whatever kind of farm work. And when all of those things was over we had to go to the woods. That's the only thing that never was over.

Every Saturday she did washin' and ironin' and I would do dishes and things. The woman paid Mama fifty cents and I didn't get nothin' for the dishes. One mornin' I went in to do the dishes and the woman had taken her wristwatch and ring and put it where she know I had to see it. I called Mom and said this ring and watch is hangin' up here. Mama said, ''Now, I didn't raise no fish. Don't you bite at everything you see.''

I never will forget one night. At my Mama's house, we always kept meal for cornbread. One night she said, ''Lord, I'm gonna cook this last bread for us to eat. This is all I got. You always said 'You never made a mouth that You didn't make a piece of bread.' I'm depending on You.'' About four o'clock that morning, somebody knocked on the door. [A neighbor] said they all gonna have their hogs killed. They give us enough meat to last us all the year. Mama said the Lord will feed us, and that's the reason I know to depend on the Lord.

I had fourteen children. Seven of them was my sister's. I was fifteen when she died. She was twenty-eight. Her request was for me and Mama to raise the children. I went away to work where they gave me seven dollars a week and room and board. As soon as I got the seven dollars I just put it in an envelope and sent it on to Mama for the kids. She could do pretty good with seven dollars. I did that for five years. When I married Presley Williams, the baby girl was the last one. I had her until she finished school.

I was seventy years old when I took in the last two boys 'cause their mother died. I got the papers for all fourteen. I had to adopt them to get them legal.

In the first year my husband made good, come out of debt, me and him bought us a horse, wagon, two mules and some. We stayed there that year and they shot at us. I would've got killed. My husband said, ''Just roll out on that side.'' So I rolled out one side of the bed and he rolled out on the other and there was a truck shootin' at us. They said they didn't want no Negroes there.

They told us, ''You better read and run. If you can't read, you better run anyhow.''

When I was married and lived in Oklahoma, my husband said, ''When I sell this crop, I'm going to take you to see your daddy.'' We got us a old Ford car that didn't have no top on it. We got there on a Sunday morning. My father's wife was in the house. When my husband hollered back to the car and say, ''Get out, honey, this where your daddy lives,'' she said, ''Daddy? The man I married ain't old enough to have no daughter. He say he didn't have no children.'' She kept on watching to see would Daddy own me or disown me. When Daddy come in, me and him both set there and cried and cried.

Rose and me was raised together. I never could understand why I was black and she was white. We's about five or six and she'd call me her little dark-skinned white girl. She said, ''I'm gonna get Priscilla white like me.'' She got the soap and washed my face, rubbed my hands. In the palm of my hand it was real light. She said, ''Mother, look, her hands are gettin' white.'' Her mother told Rose to keep on washin'. She never did try to make me feel bad.

The last time I saw Rose she was grown. We talked and cried 'bout the times we used to have fun when we was children. She said, ''I laugh to myself how me and you was tryin' to get you white. I still love you.''

My mother was 101 years old when she died. She just slept away, that's all.

Mama, I thank the Lord for her. She said if you want to go to heaven, you got to love white people. Said God love 'em, He made 'em. That was the hardest thing for me to do, love white people. When I was little I was scared of 'em. We thought white people would just kill ya, do ya mean things just because. Mama kept a tellin' us, ''I love 'em 'cause they ain't gonna keep me out of heaven.''

Leah Chase

Born January 6, 1923, in New Orleans, Louisiana

Leah Chase is a master chef in the Creole tradition. Her recipes are based on the seasonings and cooking methods she learned from her mother and still include the unique touch of fresh sassafras leaves from a tree her father planted. Her creative cuisine is the specialty of the house at Dooky Chase's, a family-owned restaurant in New Orleans with a nation-wide mailing list for gumbo to go. Chase has brought Dooky's (named for her husband) from a shop where only sandwiches and coffee were served to a restaurant that has become a legend in African American communities across the nation. She authored The Dooky Chase Cookbook *in 1990, was visiting Culinary Professor at Nicholls State University in 1996, and continues to serve on the university's Advisory Council. In 1998, Leah Chase was presented with the* Times Picayune's *Loving Cup, the greatest honor that a citizen of New Orleans can receive. She was the first black woman ever to receive the prize.*

My mother had twelve girls before she had a boy. My dad never told us that things were limited for us because we were female. He always told us, "Just work and pray and you can't go wrong." The two you had to do together.

It's amazing how people will say what you can't do today. They'll tell you, "Kids can't go to school and learn today unless they have bacon, eggs, grits, orange juice, and so on." That's as false as can be. In my day you went to school with a nice little cold biscuit that my mother, with all those children, had to make the night before because with a wood stove she would not have time in the morning. A little cold biscuit with homemade strawberry jam. And you certainly had *better* learn. We had to come home with good report cards or got whipped.

We were the poorest people in the town and we lived next to the wealthiest people in the town. So, it wasn't the racism that you felt. I was too busy fighting poverty to fight anything else.

Coming from a small town, you don't feel racism as you do maybe in a big city. I remember there was a white boy and a black boy, and they used to get in awful fights. But people didn't look at it as a black and white fight, it was just two boys fighting. They just beat the heck out of one another and called it a day.

I came back to New Orleans in 1942 when I was eighteen from Madisonville where I was reared. I got a job in a restaurant in the French Quarter, no less. I had never seen the inside of a restaurant in my life. I learned how to wait tables and I loved it. I loved that business and I used to wish all the time to own it.

When I started in this restaurant in 1946, black people had no restaurants as such. I had to battle with my mother-in-law and my father-in-law who started this restaurant with no knowledge of the business at all. I'd say, "We're going to set these tables up." And they'd say, "Oh, no, people are not going to want to use those forks if they're already on the table." They had never been on the inside of a restaurant. Nobody black had been in a restaurant because there were none to go to.

When I first started shrimp cocktail, people thought it was a drink.

It didn't dawn on me that I would cook. I came in here to be the little hostess with the mostest. But I started cooking the things I knew how to cook. When I put them on my menu, the gumbos and jambalayas, there was not one restaurant in this city serving them. The big restaurants were doing French things. Now everybody is serving everything. But they call it Cajun, and it's not Cajun, it's Creole.

All of the people who write about this food will tell you that it is a mixture of the French, the Spanish, and the African and a little Indian. Gumbo is okra in Africa. So gumbo was made with okra. The filé came by way of the American Indians who ground the sassafras leaves into powder. That's what we use in the Creole gumbo.

Creoles never ate without a good glass of wine. We grew strawberries and my daddy made the best strawberry wine. He went to his grave with the recipe. That wine was clear as a crystal. We had a glass of water and a spoon of wine. As we got older, the water got less and the wine got more. As poor as we were coming up, it was strange: no meat in the beans, but wine with the dinner.

I tell people all the time, you have to be in love with that pot. You have to put all your love in that pot. If you're in a hurry, just eat your sandwich and go. Don't even start cooking, because you can't do anything well in a hurry.

I love food. I love serving people. I love satisfying people.

For years we've had this restaurant. It's forty-seven years old. And it's only four years since we've expanded. People would come and wait the longest for food. I hated that. There is no food great enough to wait in a line for it.

Now, there were always black chefs running the show, but black women worked with them, under them. There was a black woman, an excellent pastry chef, who created a mile-high pie. The chef got the credit but it was her creation. I think that was because black women, as a rule, were not pushy, power-seeking people.

I have a cookbook copyrighted around 1901. When this old black woman cook was asked for her recipes, she said, "I'll give you the recipes, but cooking is just like religion. Rules don't no more make a cook than sermons make a saint." I always remember that.

Elizabeth Cotten

Born January, 1892, in Chapel Hill, North Carolina
Died June 29, 1987, in Syracuse, New York

Libba Cotten won a Grammy award in 1984 for her music on "Elizabeth Cotten Live!," voted the best ethnic or traditional folk recording that year. Singer, storyteller, composer, guitarist, and banjo player, she worked as a housekeeper for decades before beginning a performing career at age sixty-seven. She is the author of many songs, including the folk classic, "Freight Train," which have also been recorded by groups as diverse as Peter, Paul and Mary and the Grateful Dead. Until her death at age ninety-five, she continued to perform around the country in the three-fingered style of picking that now bears her name.

I named myself. The first day I went to school, the teacher was calling roll and everybody was called a name. My parents didn't name me. They all called me Sis, you know. So when the teacher got to me, she said, "Li'l Sis, don't you have a name? What is it?" And I just said, "Elizabeth." I don't know where I got that name. So she put it down and I started being called Elizabeth.

When I was a little girl my mother and father used to bury their meat. Rub it up and bury it in the ground and put dirt back over it like we didn't have no meat. The white people would come and take it away from us. My mother said she could hear the horses' feet coming over the bridge. And she said, "Neville, you better go to hidin' it." She'd tell him, "Hide the meat, I hear the horses' feet." He'd leave a bone where he done cut all the meat off and leave that in the meat house like the meat gone. And then he'd dig a hole and put all the meat in it. They'd come around and look for it. If he didn't hide some of it he wouldn't have none when they left.

When I was a child I went to the door and asked people if they needed somebody to work. I said, "I can wash your dishes, I can set your table, and I can sweep your kitchen and everything." And I went to work for this lady for seventy-five cents a month.

I saved my money and gave it to my mother and when she got enough we bought a guitar. I carried it home and started pluckin' on it. My mother said, "Now if you don't put that thing down, I'm gonna git ya. I gotta get to sleep and to work in the mornin'." And I'd say, "Mama, I'm gonna stop. This is the last song." And I just keep everybody awake all night. Lord have mercy. I was a nuisance, I know I was. But my mama would always say, "She's my baby. Now let her do what she wants to do. She ain't doin' nothin' wrong."

I didn't have no lessons. Not nobody teach me. I didn't know nothin'. I worked hard. I started playin' one string at a time. Get a song and get a string and just play up and down. And then I tried to play more strings into the song.

All my brothers could play. Sometimes I'd ask my brothers to show me how to make a chord on the guitar. They said, "I can't show you how to do it. You got your fingers on the wrong strings. You're playin' the left hand and you never stop pickin'. Change the strings and put your fingers on like I tell ya." I couldn't do it. I was playin' my guitar left-handed and I didn't change the strings.

I pick the tune, you know, just on the strings. That's the way I did all my songs. I reckon that's why they named it "Cotten pickin'."

I went to work for the Seeger family [which included folk singers Mike and Pete Seeger]. I did everything, cooked, washed dishes, served. One day, Michael says to me, "Elizabeth, why don't we give a little concert?" They knew I could play because I was playin' the guitar ever' minute I got. We had that concert and I stopped work then and went on out to play.

Say I'm a musician if you want to, but I didn't know one chord from another. I don't know it yet, I mean in letters. Just let me pick and sing.

I just love to sing. I love to get up before people and let 'em hear what I can do. It does me good to play my guitar. I love to entertain people, sing to 'em, talk, tell little things about me, what all I used to do. That was my pleasure to do that.

I was just glad to get the Grammy. I didn't know what the thing was. It's the honor what I loved.

Marian Anderson

Born February 27, 1902, in Philadelphia, Pennsylvania
Died April 8, 1993, in Portland, Oregon

Marian Anderson was considered the greatest contralto of her generation and one of the golden voices of the century. When she was refused permission to sing at Constitution Hall by the Daughters of the American Revolution, the President's wife, Mrs. Eleanor Roosevelt, resigned her membership in protest. Then, offered the use of the Lincoln Memorial, Miss Anderson performed outdoors before an enthusiastic crowd of 75,000 on Easter Sunday, 1939. In 1955, she became the first black soloist to sing at the Metropolitan Opera House in New York City. Her extraordinary career and the grace with which she lived it made her a respected symbol of black womanhood around the world and helped destroy racial barriers in classical music. Her autobiography, My Lord, What a Morning *was published in 1956.*

My grandmother played the organ and my two sisters and I had a trio. Our church offered a great opportunity because we had concerts there often. I found myself taken up by the people who arranged the concerts. It came to the time when I would sing alone, charging the great price of five dollars. I'd accept a dollar for myself. A dollar went to my sister next to me in age and another dollar went to my younger sister. My mother got two dollars. Then we graduated to ten dollars, and as time moved on, we moved on to a concert at a fifteen-dollar fee. That was such a big fee.

We were going to the store one day for some provisions my mother wanted, and I saw a handbill on the pavement. I looked at it and looked at it again. I said, "That looks like me." And it was. There was going to be a concert with "The Baby Contralto," me at eight or ten years old. I was taken up with that. I had never seen my picture before except at home.

I thought being a doctor would be a nice profession. But it was out of the question, because whenever I heard music, I went in that direction. In our first music class in school I learned the words to songs by hearing them in another room. When one song came, I threw back my head and yelled out, "Sleep, Polly, sleep." The teacher came with a ruler and tapped me on the back, and said, "What are you singing? The word is peacefully." Peacefully sleep, and I thought it was sleep, Polly, sleep.

When I was quite young, in my early teens, I passed by a house and somebody was playing the piano and singing. I remember getting up on the top step and I saw a woman playing the piano and singing. I got down realizing that if she could do that, I could also. I think that changed my thinking about myself and what I might do.

Mother worked by day at the Wanamaker store. When I'd come from high school, I'd usually stop in at Wanamaker's to say hello to her. She was usually digging in some corner, cleaning out. And I thought that wasn't the kind of thing she should be doing. I was sure that they were taking unfair advantage of her. It was not what I wanted for her.

At that time, I did not have a regular job. You wait until somebody asks you to give a concert. I wasn't sure that I would have five or ten dollars at the end of the week. But I thought we should take the risk [of letting me support the family].

What you don't know, you fear. It is fear that drives us to do many things that we wouldn't otherwise do. But I am a believer. I know He lives and I know He cares for me, and that is a great help with everything.

When we have a talent, very often we don't know where to go with it. We had a fine offer to sing in a nightclub, but we never had the desire to sing in a nightclub. I am not sorry the way that we went. But I feel that I could have done other things which might have taken me where I wanted to go a little earlier.

The singer Roland Hayes impressed me very much. I tried singing in my key some of the songs that he had sung at our church over the years. He sent me a song, it was a duet which he wanted me to do with him. I was in not only seventh heaven, but ninth heaven.

Eleanor Roosevelt I knew as an extraordinary person. The visit at Constitution Hall, I knew absolutely nothing about until I was already at Alexandria. There were newspaper people from all over the place and some of them were disappointed when I didn't have much to say. It was a thing for which I had wished a long, long time. I never would have pushed for another concert myself. That's why I feel that many people have been responsible for where we stand at the peak of our career. It couldn't have been done alone.

I think one of the biggest things in my life was the time I sang at the Metropolitan Opera. My mother was in the audience and she came backstage afterwards. When I hugged her, she said, "Darling, we must thank the Lord." She was a firm believer in the good things that came from above.

Sometimes you're overwhelmed when a thing comes, and you do not realize the magnitude of the affair at that moment. When you get away from it, you wonder, did it really happen to you.

I don't feel that I opened the door. I've never been a great mover and shaker of the earth. I think that those who came after me deserve a great deal of credit for what they have achieved. I don't feel that I am responsible for any of it, because if they didn't have it in them, they wouldn't be able to get it out.

Winson and Dovie Hudson

Dovie Hudson was born July 29, 1914, in Carthage, Mississippi—Died November 5, 1994
Winson Hudson was born November 17, 1916, in Carthage, Mississippi

We lived in this black community and those large families were very protective of their children, especially girls. White men would walk the trails where we had to go wash at the spring and if they caught a girl alone there, they'd just rape her. Parents was afraid to say too much about it. You might be visited by the KKK that night. There wasn't nothing they could do about it. (WH)

My mama and daddy had fourteen children, but they raised twelve. Our mother was a missionary and our father was a minister. So we were brought up very religious, singing. She can sing. I can't sing. We travel together and they say I preach and she sing. (WH)

They called us the Big Women from Leake County everywhere we'd go across the state. (WH)

My dad was brave, he had that hostility in him 'cause they hung his brother. When the Ku Klux Klans would come through here, other people would come to our house for safety. My daddy was not afraid and that taught us. We never was afraid of them. And we got people much younger than we are, just so afraid of white people right now. (WH)

We petitioned the school board to desegregate the public school. That was the first step. The petition carried fifty-two names. They took all of these names and put it up in the courthouse where everybody could see it. White people pressured all but thirteen to remove their name. Really it was six that stayed. Dovie, she was the leader. I give her credit. She was a brave woman here with ten children. (WH)

I borrowed a little money from the bank to do my planting, and they called me in at the bank. The banker says to me, "We have been mighty good to you. We lent you money." I said, "Yes, but I've been paying it back, haven't I?" He said, "Well, yes, but we have to have our money or else we're going to foreclose." I said that I wasn't going to remove my name from the petition. "You'll just have to foreclose," I said. "The stock is there when you get ready to pick 'em up." They took all I had, seven cows and one mule. (DH)

My daughters were sitting at the table here getting out their homework. And they throwed that bomb there. It knocked that window out. (DH)

They come through here putting bombs in the mailbox. I heard the bombs go off. She called me and said, "They're on their way down there." I called my boys and one got one gun and one got the other one. And just as they drove up and put the bomb in the mailbox, my boys started shooting. They just lined that car with bullets up and down. (DH)

The more they did to us, the meaner we got. (WH)

Our husbands was not as brave as we was. We had to protect our men. If my husband had've been in my place, he would not have made it, 'cause the black man has always been the target. (WH)

That voters' registration, that was something else. It took me two years to get registered. It took Dovie eighteen months. (WH)

One time we went into the courthouse and we saw a bunch of great big ol' white men clustered around the door where we had to go in and register. I say, "Dovie, they got us today." She said, "Let's go down in the basement and pray." We went down in the basement and she prayed. They said I was too mean to pray. (WH)

Dovie talked to the Lord about it. And she said, "Let's go. There's a shield over us. They can't touch us." So we walked way down the long hall. They had the door covered, and were clustered around. And do you know we walked through those men and just rubbed 'em. "Excuse me, excuse me." And they just turned their backs. (WH)

When we went in to register, they would come in and put a card down. (WH)

It was just big enough for two eyes. (DH)

It say, "The eyes of the Klan is upon you. You have been identified by the White Knights of the Ku Klux Klan." (WH)

When you go in to register, they give you a sheet of paper and a article in the Mississippi constitution. When you get through writing it, then you got to interpret it. And so you do all of this. And then I'd go back and they'd say, "The board said y'all didn't pass." I'd say, "What board?" "Well, we got a board and they said y'all didn't pass," and we'd go back again. (WH)

A lawyer from the Justice Department came here and investigated. When we went back to register, the registrar gave me this thing to fill out again, and instead of filling it out, I wrote down there, "It said what it meant and meant what it said." He say, "Well, so you passed." (WH)

We really taught them some lessons. (DH)

That's the reason we're so educated, because we taught 'em. I've never walked down the hall with a cap and gown on, but I walked down a hall in Washington and I lobbied for student loans, and I lobbied for Social Security, and I lobbied for teachers' pay raises, and I've helped you get equal pay right here in the county, so I'm the educator. (WH)

Winson and Dovie Hudson served as committed community activists in rural Mississippi for decades. They, on behalf of their children, were the first black plaintiffs to file a school desegregation suit against the state. They were also instrumental in democratizing voter registration, establishing preschool centers, and implementing nutrition programs. Although her sister has passed on, Winson Hudson, at age 83, is still a dedicated fighter for justice. She has been the president of Leake County, Mississippi, NAACP for thirty-seven years and is the recipient of multiple honors and awards in her home state. In 1997, Mrs. Hudson traveled to the Alex Haley Farm in Clinton, Tennessee to tape an account of her activities in Leake County during the Civil Rights Movement; the taping was accomplished under the auspices of the Children's Defense Fund. The Winson Gates Hudson Headstart School opened its doors in 1998.

Maya Angelou

Born April 4, 1928, in Saint Louis, Missouri

Maya Angelou has published five volumes of her autobiography, the first of which, I Know Why the Caged Bird Sings, *was nominated for a National Book Award in 1974 and aired as a television movie in 1979. An artist of wide-ranging talents, she was the first black woman director in Hollywood and has written, produced, directed, and starred in productions for stage, film, and television. In 1981, she accepted a lifetime appointment as Reynolds Professor of American Studies at Wake Forest University, Winston-Salem, North Carolina. In 1993, Angelou composed and read a poem for the first Clinton inaugural. "On the Pulse of Morning," was awarded a Grammy the following year for Best Spoken Word Album. She has also written several titles for children,* Life Doesn't Frighten Me *and* My Friendly Chicken and Me *among them, and is presently at work on a series of books about children of different cultures. The first,* Kofi and His Magic, *was published in 1996.*

I was a mute for five years. I wasn't cute and I didn't speak. I don't know what would have happened to me had I been in an integrated school. In another society, I'm sure I would have been ruled out. But my grandma told me all the time, "Sister, Mama don't care what these people say about you being a moron, being a idiot. Mama don't care. Mama know, Sister, when you and the good Lord get ready, you're gonna be a preacher."

Recently, I gave the principal speech to the National Council of Christians and Jews.

Love affords wonder. And it is only love that gives one the liberty, the courage to go inside and see who am I really.

The larger society said that I belonged to an unwelcome tribe. My feeling was, "Unwelcome to you, but my people don't say that." Which is one of the reasons black women have survived, and done better than that, thrived.

But some of us don't, and we don't know who we've lost. It's impossible to say what we've lost when we cut off one group. We are all diminished when one group is diminished. Can you imagine if this country were not so afflicted with racism? Can you imagine what it would be like if the vitality, humor, and resilience of the black American were infused throughout this country?

It seems to me that real sexism is a newly delivered message. Black women and black men know that we were stolen and sold together on the African continent. We lay spoon fashion in the filthy hatches of slave ships together. We stood upon the auction block together, were sold again together, took the lash together. There's no question of superiority. We have survived somehow together.

One of the unfortunate results of living a legendary life and dying a legendary death is that when the person is written about, more often than not he is made larger than life. The human qualities of humor, being wrong, sometimes gauche, losing, forgetting, these wonderful qualities we all have are never mentioned. The legend is taken out of the possession of the people. Every word uttered was memorable. Well, that's not true.

I don't tell everything I know but what I do tell is the truth. There's a world of difference between truth and facts. Facts can obscure the truth. You can tell so many facts that you fill the stage but haven't got one iota of the truth.

I have no modesty, none. It's a waste of time. It's a learned affectation stuck on from without. If life slams the modest person against the wall, he or she will drop that modesty quicker than a stripper will drop her G-string. What I hope I have and what I pray for is humility. Humility comes from within.

Humility says there were people before me who found the path. I'm a road builder. For those who are yet to come, I seem to be finding the path and they will be road builders. That keeps one humble. Love keeps one humble.

Being humble doesn't mean one has to be a mat. In fact, just the opposite. What it means is, I will make myself so fine that I will be of use to you, make myself useful, do what I can do, and be an instrument of God. I do believe that anybody who can't be used is useless.

I believe all the tools that have been given to me that I recognized, I have developed. They may have been given to me as crowbars and I've tried to turn them into levers.

Strictly speaking, one cannot legislate love, but what one can do is legislate fairness and justice. If legislation does not prohibit our living side by side, sooner or later your child will fall on the pavement and I'll be the one to pick her up. Or one of my children will not be able to get into the house and you'll have to say, "Stay here until your mom comes home." Legislation affords us the chance to see if we might love each other.

It is imperative that young people be told that we have come a long way, otherwise they are likely to become cynical. A cynical young person is almost the saddest sight to see, because it means that he or she has gone from knowing nothing to believing in nothing. Young people must not get to the point of saying, "You mean to tell me we had Malcolm X, Martin Luther King, Medgar Evers? You mean to tell me we had the Kennedys, we had Fannie Lou Hamer and Mary McLeod Bethune? You mean to tell me we had all these men and women and we have made no progress? Then what the hell—there is no progress to be made. It can't be made."

So it must be simultaneous—how far we have come and how far we have to go.

I'm convinced that I'm a child of God. That's wonderful, exhilarating, liberating, full of promise. But the burden which goes along with that is, I'm convinced that everybody is a child of God. The brutes and bigots, the batterers and the bastards are also children of God. And that's where the onerous burden comes in for me, as a practicing Christian, to try to keep that in mind and not grit my teeth until they break off into little stubs.

I weep a lot. I thank God I laugh a lot, too. The main thing in one's own private world is to try to laugh as much as you cry.

Septima Poinsette Clark

Born May 3, 1898, in Charleston, South Carolina
Died December 15, 1987, on Johns Island, South Carolina

Septima Clark, one of the most effective and yet unsung heroes of the civil rights movement, believed that literacy was the key to empowerment. After teaching for many years in the public schools of South Carolina, she went on to work tirelessly with the Highlander Folk School in Tennessee and the Southern Christian Leadership Conference in Georgia. With her talent for developing leadership, she established innovative citizenship schools throughout the South. She recruited hundreds of teachers who taught thousands of others to read, to register to vote, and to stand up for their rights.

*Originally appeared in Ready from Within *by Septima Clark, edited by Cynthia Stokes Brown (Navarro, CA: Wild Trees Press, 1986).*

Septima is the Latin word for seventh, and in Haiti it means sufficient. My parents named me Septima, and I wondered why, because I was not the seventh child and neither was I sufficient, because six came after me. But I got that name from an aunt down in Haiti whose name was Septima Peace, Sufficient Peace. I was supposed to be sufficient peace, but I certainly wasn't sufficient, and I don't know about the peace, because I did so many things that wasn't peaceful.*

My father came out of slavery nonviolent. He was a gentle, tolerant man. My mother was something else. She boasted that she was never a slave, but I have a feeling that somewhere down the line somebody paid her way out. My mother was born in Charleston but reared in Haiti. The English schoolteachers in Haiti did a very good job with my mother, because they taught her how to read and write. That made her the proud soul she was all her life.*

[In 1956, after being fired by the Board of Education for being a member of the NAACP] I had to go away for twenty years from Charleston. I couldn't get a job here, nowhere in South Carolina. Not only that, but the black teachers here . . . gave me a testimonial . . . and do you know that at that party my sorors would not stand beside me and have their picture made with me? If they had, they would have lost their jobs.*

I traveled by bus all over the South, visiting teachers and recruiting new ones. I always took the fifth seat from the front to test the buses. They asked me to move, but I didn't. I reminded them that we had a law now that said we could sit anywhere in the bus.*

We went into various communities and found people. I sat down and wrote out a flyer saying that the teachers we need in a citizenship school should be people who are respected by the members of the community, who can read well aloud, and who can write their names in cursive writing. These are the ones we looked for.*

We were trying to make teachers out of people who could barely read and write. But they could teach. If they could read at all, we could teach them that c-o-n-s-t-i-t-u-t-i-o-n spells constitution.*

When they saw the black people coming in to register [to vote] at the bank, the registrar would hide in a vault and pretend that registration was closed. We had a lady there who was very fair. We sent her in, and when the man came out to register her, the other black people surged in. They thought they had a white woman but she was one of us.*

They considered me a Communist, because I was following Martin Luther King. But anyone who was against segregation was considered a Communist.*

I felt that Dr. King had a dream that all people should be free. When he said "freedom," he was thinking that they should be able to do the things that they wanted to do in America. I think we're nearer. I want people to say, "This is my dream and I want it carried forth." I want that dream enforced.

In those days I didn't criticize Dr. King other than asking him not to lead all the marches. Like other black ministers, Dr. King didn't think too much of the way women could contribute. I see this as one of the weaknesses of the civil rights movement, the way the men looked at women.*

My husband had strong feelings against women and he did not think that women had the right to do anything worthwhile. As we grew up together he never, never believed that there were women who could do things. He always felt that a woman should stay in her place, in the house. I couldn't see that women should be just in the house making children, keeping house, or buying groceries. So we could not agree.

I think that the work the women did during the time of civil rights is what really carried the movement along. The women carried forth the ideas. I think the civil rights movement would never have taken off if some women hadn't started to speak up.*

Women need to grab the men by the collar and do more. That's the way I feel. We need women who will get these men by the collar and work with them. We still have a hard time getting them to see what it means to vote.

I have great belief in the fact that whenever there is chaos, it creates wonderful thinking. I consider chaos a gift.*

I'd tell the children of the future that they have to stand up for their rights. They have an idea that they can. But I feel that they are shadows underneath a great shelter and that they need to come forth and stand up for some of the things that are right.

Acknowledgments

This project owes its real life to the early encouragement and support of Raymond H. DeMoulin, General Manager of the Professional Photography Division and Vice President of EASTMAN KODAK COMPANY. When I first approached him with this proposal, Ray DeMoulin immediately understood the historical significance of the women and agreed to a major funding, without which I might never have been able to embark upon this project. This is but one of a series of major photographic works which Ray DeMoulin and Eastman Kodak have supported in recent years, projects that have added to the continual nurturing of photojournalism in this country and abroad. I believe that Ray DeMoulin's vision and Kodak's monies represent the best kind of corporate support in America of the arts, journalism, and history.

Joining in the funding of the opening exhibition at the Corcoran Gallery of Art in Washington, D.C., and of subsequent exhibitions throughout the country, is U S W E S T, a corporation in the business of communication and information systems which has sought to extend the levels of communication and information between cultures, not only in the western United States but in the country as a whole. The officers of U S W E S T have stood by that commitment by enthusiastically embracing this project. Special thank you goes to Jane Prancan, their Director of Community Affairs and Executive Assistant to the Chairman.

My desire to achieve maximum photographic quality dictated that I use large- or medium-format cameras, depending on time constraints and locations. I am grateful to VICTOR HASSELBLAD INC. and its technical director Ernst Wildi for the use of a HASSELBLAD camera system, which I used for most of the photographs. When conditions allowed, a SINAR 8 × 10 view camera was used. My appreciation goes to Ulrich Krahenbuhl, President of SINAR BRON INC., who provided not only the SINAR 8 × 10 but BRONCOLOR electronic flash equipment, which was used throughout the duration of this project. The flawless performance and durability of this equipment, which crisscrossed the country almost continuously for the better part of two years, was remarkable.

I am indebted to many people for their help and assistance, but to none more than Rich Clarkson. Early in my career he taught me what "journalism" in the word photojournalism meant. It is because of that education that this project is not just a collection of photographs. He believed in my idea and my ability to undertake it. The critical, substantial funding and support necessary to bring this project to life was organized by Rich. I remain extremely grateful for his help and friendship.

Every undertaking of this kind should be blessed with an Yvonne Easton. Yvonne joined this project while working on the news desk at *LIFE* magazine. Her role was to assist in research and scheduling. Raised in Harlem, she is both a writer and artist. Her knowledge about historical black women, along with her sensitivity and her networking ability, soon redefined her role into one that was indispensable. The assignment of bringing these women together for this book and exhibition was an immense task. Yvonne's performance in this area was a true achievement. Much of the success of this project belongs to her.

The personal prizes of new friendships have lined the path of this project. My heartfelt thanks are due especially to Maya Angelou who graciously gave her poetry, heart, and perspective in writing the foreword to this book.

John Frook, writer, educator, former News Editor of *LIFE* magazine and a close friend, contributed to this undertaking on many levels. He screened dozens of newspapers from across the country for two years and provided important suggestions for inclusions in the project. His months of work poring over the transcriptions of hundreds of hours of interviews were essential assistance to me in the editing process. I thank him for all that he has done.

Finding someone to make photographic prints who shares one's own dedication and artistic sensibilities is a match seldom achieved. I am thankful for Mary Ellen Mark who introduced me to her printer, Gary Schneider of Schneider/Erdman, a photo lab in New York City. All the photographs for both the book and the exhibition were printed by Gary Schneider, whom I've come to appreciate as a most remarkable technician and artist. The photos, which were all taken on Kodak T-Max 100 and 400 ASA films, were printed on Kodak Elite Paper.

My photographic assistants were a vital and integral component to the interviews and photographs. I am most grateful to Neale Duckworth, who assisted throughout most of this project. His involvement went far beyond just assisting; he became essential to the work. Additional assistants were Frank Atura, Gordon Edwardes, Rosanne Olsen, Howard Simmons, Julie Coburn, Frank Schaefer, and Fiona Hamilton. I would also like to thank my assistant at home in Eugene, Oregon, Mona Miksch, who made my life and this project much easier. Their talent and care added substantially.

An early and enthusiastic advisor was Jane Livingston, Associate Director of the Corcoran Gallery of Art in Washington, D.C. I have valued her advice and encouragement throughout the entire project. She has viewed the work not just as art but as American history. The exhibition formally opened at the Corcoran Gallery of Art on February 10, 1989, and traveled throughout the country under the auspices of the American Federation of Arts. I thank the AFA for their efforts in organizing the tour.

One of the surprises and joys was working with Barbara Summers on the final editing of the interviews. Her expertise and dedication were not only beneficial, they became a wonderful support system as well. I will always remain grateful to her and to Maureen Graney, my editor at Stewart, Tabori & Chang. Andy Stewart, J.C. Suarès, Jeff Batzli, Kathy Rosenbloom, Sandie Cummings, and the rest of the staff at Stewart, Tabori & Chang were most helpful and enjoyable to work with.

A sincere thank you to the hundreds of people throughout the country who contributed in their many special ways to this project, especially Michael O'Brien, Elizabeth Owen, Frank Deford, Pat Ryan, Mrs. Bud Lanker, John Loengard, Mel Scott, Bobbi Baker-Burrows, June Goldberg, Vernon Jordan, Greg Heisler, Bob Gilka, Bill Kesler, Buck Tharp, Allen Dutton, Howard Chapnick, Mary Ann Dutton, Blaine Newnham, Betsy Frampton, Dr. Peter Cary, Joanna Newnham, Tom Hardin, Ann Moscicki, Curtis Johnson, the National Coalition of 100 Black Women, Dr. Pamela Cary, Marianne Samenko, George Frampton, Peter Howe, Glory Van Scott, Liz Donegan, Felton Sealey, Jeanie Robinson, Gil Acevedo, Edwin Coleman, John Erdman, Libby Turnock, Cindy Luxton, Stacey Zaferes, Walter Newalis, David Arnold, Bevely Spurlin, Courtney Arnold, Kathy Kifer, Don Latarski, Peggy Hamlin, Lynne Lamb, Jan Gilka, McDonald Frame Shop, Chuck Whisenant, Robert Bass, Ken Mann, Robin Dictenberg, Gil Rogin, Terry Taitz, Frances Fralin, Nicole Newnham, Kenny Moore, Ron Freeman, Van Evers, John Ullman, Tom Miksch, Eve Wilkins, Mary Baker, Johnny Garry, R. Smith Schuneman, Lynn Hammersten, John Junis, David Rawcliffe, Col. Carroll Williams, Elaine Steele, Willis Edwards, Fritz Goode, Barbara Henckel, Orland R. Bulkeley, Dolly McPherson, Mildred Garris, Deloris Cunningham, Johnine Rankin, George T. Nierenberg, Jacqueline Jackson, Willie J. Smith, Ora Williams, and Marilyn Meitz.

To my family, with whom I've spent far too little time during the last two years: I'm grateful for your help, patience, and understanding.

To the seventy-six women who appear in this book and exhibition: thank you for your love, your time, and the gifts you have shared with all of us. —B.L.

Brian Lanker's photographic essays are seen most often in *LIFE* and *Sports Illustrated* magazines, where he is a contract photographer. His portrait portfolio of 1932 Olympic gold medalists received numerous awards as did his earlier career work at newspapers in Phoenix, Arizona; Topeka, Kansas; and Eugene, Oregon. He is among a group of only five photographers twice to be selected as Newspaper Photographer of the Year, a competition conducted by the National Press Photographers Association and the University of Missouri School of Journalism. He won the Pulitzer Prize for feature photography in 1973.

Maya Angelou is a multi-talented artist who writes poetry, prose, and screenplays and is also a performer, director, producer, and professor. She is best known for *I Know Why the Caged Bird Sings*, the first book in her much acclaimed five-volume autobiography, which she has also made into a television film.

Barbara Summers, a writer and editor, has published a collection of short stories entitled *Nouvelle Soul*, as well as the novel, *The Price You Pay*. Her latest book, *Skin Deep*, the history of black fashion models, is forthcoming.

THE LIBRARY
NEW COLLEGE
SWINDON

THE LIBRARY
NEW COLLEGE
SWINDON

The type in this book was set in Devinne and Torino by Trufont Typographers, Inc., Hicksville, New York. The book was printed and bound by Arnoldo Mondadori Editore S.p.A., Verona, Italy.